A HISTORY

OF

PUTNAM COUNTY

TENNESSEE

By WALTER S. MCCLAIN

Chapter Eight by QUIMBY DYER

Southern Historical Press, Inc.
Greenville, South Carolina

This volume was reproduced from
An 1925 edition located in the
Publisher's private Library

All rights reserved. No part of this publication may be reproduced,
stored in a retrieval system, transmitted in any form, posted
on to the web in any form or by any means without
the prior written permission of the publisher.

Please direct all correspondence and orders to:

www.southernhistoricalpress.com
or
SOUTHERN HISTORICAL PRESS, Inc.
PO BOX 1267
375 West Broad Street
Greenville, SC 29601
southernhistoricalpress@gmail.com

Originally published: Cookeville, TN. 1925
ISBN #0-89308-873-0
All rights Reserved.
Printed in the United States of America

TABLE OF CONTENTS

		PAGE
Introduction		1
Chapter I.	The Pioneers	3
Chapter II.	Old Landmarks	25
Chapter III.	Putnam County Formed	44
Chapter IV.	Towns and Villages	70
Chapter V.	Social Development	88
Chapter VI.	Industrial Development	110
Chapter VII.	Geological	125
Chapter VIII.	Biographical	129

A HISTORY OF PUTNAM COUNTY

INTRODUCTION

Ramsey's "Annals of Tennessee" and Putnam's "History of Middle Tennessee," both early and authoritative works on pioneer times in this State, have little to say of the region we now know as Putnam County. Obviously, there are many traditions of intense local interest which are of too great value to be abandoned to oblivion, even though they may not be of sufficient general appeal to deserve mention in a history of the State. Every county, therefore, should largely preserve its own history, in which should be definitely fixed its early settlement, its outstanding events and accomplishments, and, above all, faithful tribute to men and women of worth and distinction. We shall endeavor to perform this service for Putnam County.

The writer offers no apology for the deficiencies of this work, believing that they will be largely overcome in future editions. This is merely a beginning, to which others may add. It is particularly unfortunate that we are without more reliable information concerning the early settlement of this county, but it is to gather up such fugitive bits of history as may be gleaned from our oldest citizens and their family papers that this belated record is attempted.

We acknowledge our indebtedness to numerous friends who have so generously assisted us in the collection of data and who have otherwise given valuable aid in the difficult undertaking. Especially helpful were the school-girl essays of three young ladies. We refer to the "Early History of Cookeville," by Miss Anne Robinson; "Buck's College," by Miss Liza Anderson (Mrs. Bedford Morgan), and "History of Cookeville," by Miss Delia Gentry.

Mr. Ernest H. Boyd has freely given us the benefit of his extensive acquaintance throughout the county, and Mr. Jere Whitson, long prominent in public affairs, has likewise assisted us materially. To Mr. E. E. Dorman, who came here with the Nashville & Knoxville railroad as one of its first engineers, we are indebted for most of the data concerning that epochal enterprise.

Taken as a whole, the matter presented in this little volume is largely new and original. We know of no other publication covering this particular field—else we might have copied copiously, after the fashion of historians generally. In spite of its evident imperfections, we trust that the History of Putnam County may not only prove interesting reading for this generation, but that it may also serve to fix important local events for the convenient conideration of future historians.

Cookeville, Tenn., May 15, 1925.

WALTER S. McCLAIN.

A HISTORY
OF
PUTNAM COUNTY
TENNESSEE

CHAPTER ONE

THE PIONEERS

Tennessee history begins with the log cabin of William Bean, the first white settler on the Watauga River, in 1769. For many years the "Watauga Settlement" was the rendezvous for all adventurous spirits headed for the unknown and perilous West. Here the wagons gathered from Virginia and the Carolinas, and at frequent intervals large parties or wagon trains, escorted by small detachments of soldiers, would fare forth on the Western trail.

The first road to the West was the Wilderness Road, blazed out by Daniel Boone. Its course was slightly north of west from the Watauga Settlement, by way of Cumberland Gap, to a place in Kentucky called Boonesboro, where a fort was completed in 1775. James Robertson, the founder of Nashville, led his party of settlers over this road to a point north of the present city of Nashville. Here he turned south, crossed the Cumberland River on the ice, and established a settlement, first called Nashboro. This was the winter of 1779-80, known as the "cold winter." By 1788 the Cumberland Road had been extended from Campbell Station in Knox County across the mountain and on to Nashville.

Just who was the first white man to settle in the favored spot we now call Putnam County seems to be lost in the obscurity of the Past. But one day, before any road had been marked out, some paleface scout, working his way deeper and deeper into the mysterious West, must have stood upon the western brow of the Cumberland Plateau and gazed in wonder upon the hills and valleys of the middle division of our county! If tradition is true, it was a vast panorama—a gorgeous view unobstructed by forests,—an undulating plain covered with tall grass of a species now unknown to us. But this first-comer, this lord of the wilderness, left no record of his impressions, and all that we know is that he, and many others after him, pressed on farther and farther toward the setting sun, in search, no doubt, of some great river with its rich bottom lands, its easy transportation and outlet to regions yet unknown.

But years after other pioneers came and stopped to build their humble habitations. To them it was a goodly land—a land of fine water, plenty of game and but few signs of the dreaded Indian. These early settlers preempted the rich coves and choice bits of land along the creeks, erected with their own hands such houses as they were able, and in loneliness and toil laid deep and sure the foundations of our civilization. To forget these heroic men and women through whose industry and self-denial we have grown great and prosperous would be sordid ingratitude. To visualize their achievements, to bring to mind once more their homely

A HISTORY OF PUTNAM COUNTY

virtues, to call them by name as we recount their deeds— this is but a feeble tribute, but it should not be longer delayed.

In his "History of Middle Tennessee," published in the early fifties, Putnam says: "The pioneers of the Watauga and the Sewanee (Cumberland) had their trials and proved themselves rich in virtues. Like gold in the alembic, they passed through the refiner's fire, leaving the dross in deposit or cast away. Our immediate forefathers were these adventurers. Not long have they slept in the dust of death."

The early pioneers traveling westward over the Walton Road, naturally settled along this highway, usually at intervals of from two to five miles apart. Those coming later struck out deeper into the wilderness, north or south of the main road, some going over into Sinking Cane, Spring Creek, Roaring River, and even as far as the Cumberland, while those who turned southward were attracted by the fertile lands of the Calf Killer, Falling Water and Caney Fork. The rich coves along the base of the Cumberland Mountain furnished many fine farms.

Old settlers tell us that a century ago the middle section of our county was a prairie, covered with tall grass, furnishing pasturage to great herds of buffalo, deer and wild horses. No doubt this came about as a result of annual fires, purposely set by the Indians to bring about this very condition. Early historians agree that the territory bounded by the Tennessee and Cumberland rivers was once a common hunting ground for several bordering tribes, no one of whom laid any special or exclusive claim to it. The Cherokees on the east, the Creeks on the south and the Chickasaws on the west all hunted here—and sometimes fought— but no villages of any consequence were found here by the early explorers.

A HISTORY OF PUTNAM COUNTY

The first settlement in the eastern end of the county seems to have been in the vicinity of Standing Stone (now Monterey), where about a dozen families located within a radius of six or eight miles of that well-known point, during the first quarter of the last century.

About the year 1800, Alexander Officer, grandfather of W. B. Ray, enroute from Virginia to the West, located at a place a few miles east of Standing Stone, somewhat by accident. A sick horse necessitated a few days' stop, and after looking around a bit he decided to remain permanently. He died a few years later, leaving a large family. After some years, his widow married Dudley Hunter and removed to the Dry Valley.

John Whittaker, of North Carolina, settled in what is now the suburbs of Monterey, not far from 1800, and built the old log house in which his son Jefferson lived a long life. This house is still standing.

James Clark built his home on a high point near the present railroad station of Bilbrey, owning a large tract of land extending back to Standing Stone. One of his daughters married Jefferson Whittaker.

Matthias Welch came from North Carolina about 1830 and settled near the head of Falling Water.

Abraham Ford, of North Carolina, opened up what is known as the Blaylock place about 1835.

In 1818 a man named Sehon kept a tavern or stand on the Walton Road three and one-half miles west of Standing Stone. President Andrew Jackson and other eminent men were entertained there as they were enroute to and from Washington. W. B. Ray remembers hearing his grandmother, who was a Sehon, tell about watching President Jackson hold his watch for the cook to boil his eggs by. Also, how many times when she would be out looking for chestnuts she would find one or more bears nosing around after some toothsome nuts

At a slightly later day, probably 1820, Augustus Lee settled on the Walton Road, two miles west of Standing Stone. He was the grandfather of John W. Welch.

Leonard Ray, great-grandfather of W. B. Ray, opened up a farm three miles north of the Walton Road, about 1819.

About 1824 Henry Verble came from North Carolina and settled two miles east of Standing Stone, but later was attracted by the richer lands in the Sinking Cane, where he entered a large tract.

In 1825, Israel Shaver and Thomas Dyer located and established permanent homes in the vicinity of Meadow Creek.

Samuel Callahan settled in Sinking Cane, north of Standing Stone. He was something of a politician, and at one time was a member of the Legislature.

Henderson Tudor came from North Carolina at a very early date, and settled west of Standing Stone. Evidently, he was an Indian scout, since he was famous for following trails, and even his name was changed to "Henderson Trailer." His old home place is still known locally as the "Old Trailer's Place."

Vinet Henry, veteran of the War of 1812, and an Indian fighter, settled near the head of Board Valley about the year 1825.

John Henry came from North Carolina in 1812, and located at the head of the Calf Killer, his lands embracing the beginnings of that noted stream, named, according to tradition, for an Indian chief. His first habitation was a log pen thatched with cane, which grew everywhere in profusion.

A HISTORY OF PUTNAM COUNTY

Among the earliest to settle at the foot of the mountain, (three and a half miles east of Cookeville), was William Quarles, a Revolutionary soldier, who, with his large family, and several slaves, left his home in Bedford County, Virginia, and after a full month of travel reached his destination on Christmas day, 1809. Soon White Plains came into existence, with a general store, blacksmith shop, and post office, all widely patronized. The first court ever held for many miles around convened in this blacksmith shop, with Judge Quarles, by special appointment, presiding. This worthy and enterprising citizen was assassinated on a lonely road a few miles from his home by some outlaw, who was never apprehended. He left a large family, from whom many who bear the name Quarles, Burton, Hawes, Hughes, Little, and Snodgrass, trace their ancestry. One son-in-law, Adam Huntsman, was a prominent lawyer in West Tennessee, and had the added distinction of defeating the renowned Davy Crockett for Congress.

About 1820 Thomas Barnes came from North Carolina and opened up the farm now owned by J. B. Dowell, known from Civil War times as the Tom Pointer place. Mr. Barnes' grants covered several square miles. He raised a family of twenty children, the youngest of whom, Mrs. Martha Cooper, is still living. A son, John Barnes, settled on the Sparta road at an early date. Other descendants have been prominent in affairs in and around Cookeville, and will be given due notice elsewhere.

Peter Smith settled in what is now the Fifteenth civil district, before Tennessee became a state. His son, John Smith, born 1794, died 1872, lived his long and useful life in that section of the county. He was the grandfather of Milton Owen, deceased, and Mrs. L. B. Hatfield, of near Algood. His was the first grave at the old Smith's Chapel graveyard.

Calvin Crook, 94, and for nearly seventy years a leading citizen of the southern section of the county, but now residing just across the Falling Water in White County, tells us that his great-grandfather, John Crook, and his grandfather, also named John, came from North Carolina in the early years of the last century and settled on Pigeon Roost Creek, one on either side, on nice elevations about a quarter of a mile north of Falling Water. His grandfather on his mother's side, Samuel Brown, came from Ireland a few years later and settled near by. One of his daughters married John Crook, 3rd, father of Calvin.

Isaac Buck, born in 1800, settled on the first bench of the mountain, two miles east of White Plains, in the year 1820. Just married, he came with his young bride to the new country to open up a farm of some six hundred acres, Mr. Buck's father came from Germany when a young man, and settled in Pennsylvania. The family name was Bach. Isaac had received every educational advantage of his day, and being licensed to preach, he soon became pastor of Salem church, which he served faithfully for many years. In 1849 Mr. Buck purchased 140 acres of land about one mile east of Cookeville and soon after, associated with his oldest son, Jonathan, began preparations for the erection of a large school building, a description of which we give elsewhere.

Pleas Randolph came from North Carolina in 1825, and located near the present village of Brotherton, on the first bench of the mountain.

Charles Huddleston, with two brothers, Dave and John, and a man named Flanagin, came from Rutherford County, North Carolina, in 1811, arriving here on March 29th. Charles Huddleston bought out an earlier settler named Mitchell, one mile east of Salem church, known as the Jor-

A HISTORY OF PUTNAM COUNTY

dan Huddleston place, and now owned by a great-grandson, B. M. Huddleston. Charles Huddleston's oldest son, Isaac, settled in Rock Spring Valley in the lower end of the county, about 1830. A large pear tree on the old Huddleston place is known to be more than one hundred and thirty years old. It is about two feet in diameter, and bore some fruit last year, according to Mr. B. C. Huddleston.

Dave Huddleston settled on a hill near Salem, later the Lewis Huddleston farm, now owned by Lee Huddleston.

John C. Huddleston settled on the mountain above Dry Valley.

The Mr. Flanagin mentioned above was the first to be buried at the Salem graveyard.

Samuel Matheny and John Anderson Matheny, sons of Elijah Matheny, of Roane County, settled in the Fifteenth civil district at an early date, probably 1835.

Matthew Sims came to this county in 1812, from Cumberland Gap. The date is fixed by the fact that his son, Martin, born in 1800, was twelve years old when they came. Martin Sims was a prominent figure in the early history of this section and was a recognized leader in many worthy undertakings.

Jonathan Scott came from Virginia in 1808, and settled in the section now known as Ditty, then White County, in the second year after its formation. His relatives quote him as saying that many drivers, fearing to trust their wagon brakes down the mountain, would cut trees of considerable size and hitch them on behind to retard the speed.

John Allison, Revolutionarry soldier, came from Boonesborough, Orange County, North Carolina, in 1807, and settled six miles south of Baxter when his son, Joseph (Mine Lick), was six years old. When this son reached his majority the father gave him a little flea-bitten gray pony.

With this as his only start he entered land, cleared a field, and built a cabin. The pony was hitched under a tree that winter. "Uncle Mine Lick," as he was familiarly known to the people, had a fund of information gained largely by contact with Nature, and many of his original and eccentric sayings and doings are current legend for miles around his old home.

Robert Harris came from Virginia in 1820 and located three and one-half miles south of Baxter. He had three sons—Jordan, Joseph and Jack.

David Patton, and son, Samuel, came from Virginia and settled at the old Patton place, about 1818.

Barnett Richardson, of Roanoke, Virginia, settled near Baxter about 1818. He had two sons—Barnett and Caleb.

Robert Gentry came from North Carolina in 1815 and settled in the Mine Lick country. The large Gentry family descended from this pioneer.

William Thomas came from South Carolina in 1775 and located five miles southeast of Silver Point, on what is now known as the Asbury Thomas farm. He followed his sweetheart, Sallie Green, here, stealing her out and marrying her against her parents' wishes.

Richard (Dickie) Herren came from North Carolina about 1780 and entered some two thousand acres of land on Mine Lick Creek.

Joseph Roberts, of North Carolina, settled on Mine Lick around 1790, on what is now known as the Gale Herren farm.

William Barnett Kemp, also from North Carolina, located on Cane Creek about 1775, entering what is now known as the Roe Gracey farm.

Reuben Braswell came from North Carolina to the Mine Lick country about the year 1824.

Samuel Maxwell came from North Carolina in 1811 and

settled in the vicinity of Baxter. From his five sons—Amos, Gordon, Samuel, Jack and David—have descended the large Maxwell family of that section.

Abraham Buck and Jonathan Buck followed their preacher brother, Isaac, to the wilderness in the early years of the last century. Jonathan located and lived for many years just west of the Buck College site but in his later years moved to what is now known as the Pate Pointer place, where he was fatally burned in the destruction of his house. Abraham Buck entered land and settled northwest of Cookeville on the farm now owned by Esqire Harvey Shipley. A grandson, Dr. J. F. Dyer, has practiced medicine in Cookeville for almost fifty years.

Thomas Buck, father of Isaac, Jonathan, Sr., and Abraham, came to Putnam county after his boys had located. He is buried at the family cemetery on the old homestead of Enoch Buck, son of Isaac.

Michael Moore came from North Carolina in 1823 and entered land on and around Pilot Knob, south of Cookeville. His son, Hampton, was an early citizen and business man of this section. His place was known more recently as the Andrew Harpole farm, now owned by Mrs. Margaret Wright.

John Welch, of North Carolina, settled two miles southeast of Cookeville about 1820, entering the land known many years ago as the Wash Terry place, but more recently as the Dave Bullock farm.

John Bohannon, father of Pleasant Bohannon, came from Virginia over the Walton Road as far as the present site of Cookeville and then turned southeast and found a location that pleased him in the Dry Valley, being one of the first settlers in that valley. This was about 1820.

Simeon Shanks, of Virginia, entered a large tract of land

and came to the new country in 1835, locating near his father-in-law, Craven Maddux.

Silas Taylor came from Bedford County, Virginia, about 1830 and settled on the Walton Road not far from the home of his friend Thomas Holladay, who had preceded him here some four or five years. Henry C. Taylor, the oldest child, was about thirteen years old. The Taylors and Holladays had been neighbors back in Virginia and their demonstrative meeting in the wilds of their new home made a lasting impression upon the youth, who never forgot how the men embraced and shed tears of joy.

William McDonald, an English emigrant, settled with his large family on Indian Creek, about the year 1780, before the Walton Road. An older son, Hal, fought with Jackson at New Orleans and in the Indian Wars. Other children went to the far West, but the youngest, Porter and King, remained at the old homestead. King McDonald, born in 1810, is survived by his youngest son, M. T. McDonald. Andrew, son of Porter McDonald, is now ninety years of age and resides where he was born on the old place.

Boaz Ford, of Virginia, came over the Walton Road in 1824 and located near old St. Mary's, south of Chestnut Mound. While just outside the present limits of our county, Mr. Ford's activities were mainly identified with Putnam County history. In Virginia his farm adjoined that of Thomas Jefferson with whom he was well acquainted. His son, Charles R., fourteen years old at the time of the removal, became one of the early and foremost citizens of Cookeville.

John McCaleb came from Orange County, N. C., in 1824, and settled on Cane Creek, on the farm now owned by Roe Howell. His father was killed in the Revolutionary War. His son, S. M. McCaleb, was a Captain in the Civil

War.

William Allison, also from Orange County, N. C., settled on Cane Creek, at an early date, on the farm now owned by Alfred Maxwell. His son, Joseph, (known as "Hog Joe," on account of owing as many hogs), lived on the Walton Road.

James Robinson, James Scarbrough and Ned Ellems, three hardy pioneers from North Carolina, settled on the Calf Killer between the years 1800 and 1805. There was no store nearer than Nashville. Robinson and Scarbrough quarried out some hard sand stone for burrs and set up a small corn mill on Mill Creek. This was the first mill in the eastern end of the county. The water troughs were dug out of logs.

John Robinson, also from North Carolina, located in the England Cave, southeast of the Calf Killer.

James Stamps came from Virginia in the early years of the last century and settled near the head of the Calf Killer. A young son, Sandford, born there in 1811, was in his early manhood a pioneer and leading citizen of Stamp's Cove.

Major Richard F. Cooke, for whom Cookeville was named, was born in Culpepper County, Virginia, January 8, 1787. He was brought up mainly in Greenville District, S. C., and emigrated to Maury County, Tenn., in 1810, and two years later opened up the farm now known as the Thomas Holman place three miles from Double Springs, on the Gainesboro-Sparta road, comprising then several thousand acres. Maj. Cooke was an officer in Woolfork's Battalion under General Jackson. He was twice a member of the State Senate. He died Oct. 15, 1870.

Captain Jack Walker was the pioneer who settled at a very early date the Allison place on the Walton Road, known later as the Isbell place.

A HISTORY OF PUTNAM COUNTY

Job Morgan came from North Carolina about 1801 and settled on Spring Creek, then in the newly formed county of Jackson. He was the grandfather of the late Gen. George H. Morgan, prominent in Putnam county affairs.

James Peek from Virginia established his home on Spring Creek at a very early date, in the section known locally as "Little Putnam."

John Burroughs, an English emigrant, came from North Carolina in 1830 and entered land now known as the Maddux place in the 15th. Civil District. He died at the advanced age of 94, and his wife reached 96.

Jesse Phillips, of Scotch extraction, came by the way of North Carolina and settled near the old Martin Sims place in the 15th. District. This was about 1830.

William Mills, also from North Carolina, entered land three miles south-west of Cookeville back in the first quarter of the last century. His son, Billie, well-known and highly-esteemed, reared a large family at the old home place.

Elijah Ellis came from Orange County, N. C., in 1819, and located on Cane Creek. He had three sons—Elijah, Lindsey, and Wootson.

Joe Allison came from North Carolina about 1820 and opened up the placce now owned by Abe Mitchell. His son, Donaldson, was a colonel in the Confederate Army.

Alexander Madden, also from North Carolina, settled at what is now known as the Williford place, on Cane Creek, about 1820.

Daniel Brown came from North Carolina in 1830 and entered land north of the Walton Road, in the vicinity of the present village of Bloomington. This son, Jesse, died in 1914 at the age of 95, having been a Missionary Baptist preacher for more than seventy years.

Thomas Holladay came from Bedford County, Virginia,

in the year 1830, and settled north of the Walton Road, on Indian Creek, of Cumberland River. Most of this fine body of land is still owned by his descendants. His children were: John, Joseph, Betsy Hubbard, Caroline Pate, Stephen and William. His second marriage was to Agnes, sister of Joseph Jared, and their children were T. C. Holladay, Rev. J. A. Holladay, and Fannie, wife of Moses Jared. O. K. Holladay, of Cookeville, is a great-grand son of this pioneer through John and his son, William. Thomas Holladay probably introduced tobacco culture in this county. He and his sons loaded many barges with tobacco and floated them down the Cumberland and Mississippi to New Orleans, walking back the greater part of the way.

Craven and Betsy Maddux came from Virginia with their large family in 1835 and located on the Walton Road, at what is now known as the Lee place near Baxter. Their children were: Margaret, William, Redmond, Addison, Jane, Snowden Horton, Thomas, Silas, Fannie and George.

John Lee came from Virginia in 1820 and entered land in the vicinity of Double Springs.

Ivins Bartlett and Sampson Williams were the earliest settlers in "Little Putnam," entering farms there in the year of 1825.

Mark Whittaker settled on the mountain east of Dry Valley on land entered by him in 1834 and known in recent years as the William Phifer place.

Lee Sadler of Virginia located on Martin's Creek in 1820.

Dudley Hunter, of Virginia, was one of the earlier settlers in Dry Valley, his grants dating back to 1810. Daniel Boone was his mother's uncle, her father being a brother of the famous hunter.

Jordan Harris entered land on Mine Lick Creek in the year 1826.

William Boyd, of Virginia, but later from North Carolina, settled near Knoxville, this State, where he resided until his death. His son, John Boyd, born in North Carolina Dec. 9, 1777, and Elizabeth Leath, born in Virginia, Aug. 29, 1785, were married in Anderson county, Tenn., Dec. 16, 1801, and at once set out to locate in the new Cumberland country.

John Boyd entered a large tract of fine farming land in Rock Spring Valley, now the 11th civil district of Putnam county, and erected a large two-story log house, weatherboarded and ceiled throughout with hand-made lumber--an unusual house in its day. In this house John and Elizabeth Boyd reared their large family of fourteen children—seven sons and seven daughters—thirteen of whom lived to marry and rear families of their own. John Boyd volunteered in the War of 1812, in Capt. John Sutton's company of Tennessee Militia, and fought at New Orleans under Gen. Andrew Jackson. He has honorably discharged April 10, 1815, and returned to his family. He died August 20, 1837, in his sixtieth year.

Elizabeth Leath Boyd survived her husband 45 years, dying in 1882, at the remarkable age of 97. She retained great physical and mental vigor almost to the end of her life. She was intensely religious and for more than 80 years devoted each Friday to fasting and prayer, and was a leading member of the Pleasant Grove church. During the dark days of the Civil War Mrs. Boyd was strongly Southern in her sympathies and, having great strength of character, she was able to render substantial aid to her friends and neighbors by meanss of personal appeals in their behalf to Col. William B. Stokes, Federal Commander, stationed at Carthage, who was her cousin. Although she was 76 years old at the beginning of the war, she made

A HISTORY OF PUTNAM COUNTY

numerous trips to Carthage and her appeals were never in vain. She died in 1882 in the house erected by her husband about eighty years before.

After the death of John Boyd his son, Jefferson W. Boyd, purchased the interests of his brothers and sisters and continued to reside at the old home until his death in 1891. A part of the dwelling erected about 120 years ago is still standing and is owned and occupied by Prof. John J. Boyd, youngest son of Jefferson W. Boyd.

Of the thirteen children of John and Elizabeth Boyd, four married and settled in Putnam county—John C., Alexander, Jefferson W., and Bransford.

John C. Boyd married Martha Holladay. They are survived by one son, James A. Boyd, of Baxter, a Confederate veteran and a highly esteemed citizen.

Alexander Boyd married Leitha Evans. He was deputy under Sheriff Robinson Dyer, before the civil war, and carried the first prisoner from Putnam county to the State penitentiary. He also was a Confederate soldier.

Jefferson W. Boyd married Mary Jared, daughter of Moses Jared. They are survived by two sons and a daughter—John J. Boyd, of this county, Dr. W. M. Boyd, of Jackson county, and Miss Matilda Boyd. Two sons—Alvin W. and Houston S. Boyd, now dead,—were prominent lawyers of the Cookeville bar. Jefferson W. Boyd was a gallant Confederate soldier, was desperately wounded in battle, and spent many months in the Rock Island Federal prison.

Bransford Boyd married Eliza Jared. He was in the Confederate army and died of measles at Camp Trousdale. His widow died about twenty years ago. The last surviving child, George W. Boyd, died a few months ago at his home near Buffalo Valley.

A HISTORY OF PUTNAM COUNTY

The Jared family is one of the oldest and largest in the county. William Jared, born in Virginia in 1765, was the first pioneer of the name, coming over the Walton Road in 1810. He died at his home on Indian Creek in 1827. His sons, progenitors of large families, were Moses, Samuel, William, Joseph and John. A daughter, Ruth Brown, also left many decendants.

Joseph Jared, brother of William, emigrated from Virginia about the same time and located his farm on the ridge at a point known as the Low Gap. One of his sons was the late Josiah Jared, who was for many years one of the most prominent citizens of the county.

John Jared, the last surviving son of William Jared, died at an advanced age about twenty-five years ago. He was the grand father of Wirt and Walter Jared, prominent business men of Buffalo Valley.

Moses Jared married Malinda Byrne. Their home was on the farm now known as the J. P. Nichols place. They had one son, Moses, and three daughters—Elizabeth, wife of David H. Nichols; Mary, wife of Jefferson W. Boyd; and Rhoda, wife of Adolphus Young.

William Jared, Jr., was a Methodist minister. After middle life he disposed of his farm on Indian Creek and located near Sparta, where he is buried. The White County Jareds are his descendants.

The late William Jared, of Cookeville, was a grand-son of Samuel Jared, and Esq. F. H. Jared, of Gentry, is a grand-son of Joseph Jared.

Joe H. Jared, of Gentry, bears his grand-father's name. T. C. Holladay, of Cookeville, is also a grandson of the pioneer, Joseph Jared. Another grandson was the late Capt. William Ensor, progenitor of the large Ensor family of this county.

The Jared family has been actively identified with public affairs in this section for more than a century, and is in every respect, an excellent family, characterized by intelligence, integrity and frugality. Closely related to the Jareds are the Byrnes, Nichols, Holladays, Boyds, Ensors, Huddlestons, Madduxs, Leftwitches, and other large families of the Western division of the county.

Jesse Kuykendall came from Georgia in 1816 and located near Warren's Chapel, but later moved to the headwaters of Blackburn's Fork. His children were Matthew, Peter, Young, Noah, Elizabeth and Mary.

James Terry came from East Tennessee about 1815 and settled on the farm now owned by his grand-son, J. W. H. Terry. His children were William, Joseph, Frank, Curtis, James, John, Nancy, Sallie, Prudie, Rhetta, Lucy and Polly.

John Dowell, also from East Tennessee, came about the same date (1815) and located about half a mile from his friend Terry. His children were Martin, Hickman, Betty, Emma, Clara, and America.

Joseph Hunter, of Virginia, entered land in Dry Valley in the years 1807-24-28.

Nathan Bartlett was probably the earliest settler in the Dry Valley, his grants being a little older than those of his nearest neighbor, Joseph Hunter.

Robert Holladay settled on the Walton Road about 1830, at Pekin post office, known later as Pond Spring.

William Hawes, came from Virginia with his father-in-law, William Quarles, in 1809, and built his home near the spring on the farm owned by W. R. Nichols, two miles south of Algood. His son, Daniel, was a well known merchant of ante-bellum days.

Jacob Hyder, William Rodgers and Samuel Madewell, all

of English descent, came from Virginia about the year 1810. They left the Walton Road near Buck Mountain and carried their household effects on their shoulders into the wilderness at the head of Falling Water. From these pioneers descended the large families of their respective names. A log-house built by Jacob Hyder, more than a century ago, is today occupied by a great grandson. Several children emigrated to the far West, but one son, Joseph D. Hyder, remained at the old home place, about three miles below the head of Falling Water. Rodgers and Madewell settled above the Hyder place. Jesse Rogers, son of the pioneer, had a stand on the Walton Road, a little east of Buck Mountain.

William C. Bullington came to this country from Virginia in 1810, one of the very early emigrants. He settled north-west of the present town of Cookeville, in what is now called the Shipley neighborhood. Of four sons, two— Josiah and Henry, located homes near their birthplace, and two others—John and Tyre—settled on the Walton Road, a few miles west of Cookeville.

.... Caruthers came from North Carolina in the early years of the last century and settled near what was later known as the Marchbanks neighborhood. He was an expert blacksmith, as have been nearly all of his male descendants. The children of his son, Joseph, were Stephen, Benjamin, John, Emma, Haywood, Margaret and Joseph.

Hugh Wallace, of North Carolina, the progenitor of the large Wallace family, settled not far from Silver Point about 1820, and died about 1860.

John Ensor came from Virginia to Rock Spring Valley in 1824. He married Ruth, oldest daughter of Joseph Jared. He was the father of Capt. William Ensor and grandfather of John L. Ensor and Dr. L. D. J. Ensor, deceased.

A HISTORY OF PUTNAM COUNTY

Hyram Brown, born March 10, 1790, came from North Carolina at a very early date and settled first on Cane Creek, where he married Mary Ellis. About 1840 he moved to the place now owned by his grandson, Claude Brown. His wife died in 1850, and he later married Hettie Bartlett. Brown's Mill Church was named for this pioneer.

William Marchbanks, of South Carolina, located near Turkey Creek, east of Algood, at a very early date. He had five sons and two daughters—Martin, Burton, Albert, Ridley, Judge A. J., Jane and Sallie. Judge Marchbanks served on the bench for twenty years before the Civil War. The children of Burton Marchbanks were Columbus, William, Frank, Burton, Jr., and Belle.

Jeremiah Whitson came from Kentucky at an early date, probably 1815, and located on what was later known as the Joe Breeding place. His children were, Reuben, John, Miah, Betty, Sallie and Jane.

John Watson came to America from Scotland in 1778. His son, John Saul Watson, married Lucy Smith, a first cousin of Joseph Smith, founder of the Mormon Church. Two of their sons, Thomas Townson Watson and John S. Watson, were early pioneers in the Third Civil District of this county.

Joshua Bartlett, another early settler in Buffalo Valley, located just below the Jones'. His sons were Ned, Mit, Joe and Henry.

Joseph McKee settled on the Young prong of Indian Creek at a very early date. He had two daughters—Edoeden and Illiod. The latter married Henry Bartlett.

Adam Hyder, came from Virginia in 1810, and settled on the mountain, not far from the Cumberland County line.

Patsy Embry entered land on the south fork of Mine Lick Creek in 1824.

A HISTORY OF PUTNAM COUNTY

James, Matthew and Joseph McKinley emigrated from Virginia about 1815. The latter went to California, Matthew settled near Granville, while James located for awhile on Martin's Creek, and in 1817 married Eliza Bates. In 1820 this young couple moved to the Walton Road to the place known later as Mount Richardson. Their twelve children were Fleming, Isaac, John, Lemuel, James, Robert, Morena, Sarah, Jane, Mary, Elizabeth and Martha. This pioneer citizen died Feb. 5, 1839, and his wife passed away in March 1871. Two sons, James and Robert, lived on at the old home until their death in 1918. The McKinley place was a famous old stand and has been in the hands of this family for over a hundred years.

John Grime, born in Ashe County, N. C., Aug. 24, 1809, was an early settler and prominent citizen of the Eighth Civil District of this county. He owned several hundred acres of land, and was a member of the County Court and a pioneer Baptist. He was the father of Rev. J. H. Grime, a Baptist minister of Lebanon. Rev. Sam Edwards, pastor of the Cookeville Baptist Church, is another descendant. Squire Grime was a large slave holder, but when the Civil War came on he stood for the Union, making a speech against secession at the old Bunker Hill muster ground. Because of his opposition to the guerrillas he found it necessary to make a temporary home in Kentucky. He returned to his farm after the war. He was a well-informed and public-spirited citizen, and when "stump-speakers" came around, urging the issuance of bonds by the State for railroads, etc., he made it a point to answer them very effectively and to the satisfaction of his neighbors.

Years before the Civil War, before there were even villages in the territory that was to be Putnam County, there were many fine and comparatively populous communities. Around Standing Stone were the Rays, Whittakers, Welches, Clarks, Sehons, Lees and others. On the Calf Killer were the Verbles, Johnsons, Henrys, Officers and many others. At the western foot of the mountain, on the Walton Road, was White Plains, around which gathered the descendants of the pioneer William Quarles—the Quarles, Burtons, Hawes, Hughes—with the descendants of Isaac Buck near by. The Marchbanks settlement, a little north of the present village of Algood, was another fine old neighborhood. Here were Marchbanks, McKinneys, Lyles, Adkinsons, Carrs, Wards, Caruthers. In the vicinity of Salem Church and campground the Huddlestons predominated, with a few Barnes, Bohannons and Moores. In the Dry Valley were Hunters, Hyders, Bartletts, Browns, Watsons, Jacksons, Bohannons, Walkers, etc. Over in what is now the 15th Civil District, were principally Matheneys, Smiths, Phillips and Sims, and around Smyrna Church were Terrys, Dowells, Kuykendalls and others. In the vicinity of Blackburn's Fork were Dyers, Pippins, Bullingtons, Kuykendalls. In the Cane Creek country were Taylors, Whites, Maddens, Kemps, Ellis', Crooks, etc. Mine Lick settlement included mainly Maxwells, Allisons, Gentrys, Thomases, Harrises, Pattons and Herrins. Buffalo Valley was the home of the Jones', Bartletts, Wallaces, and others. The rich Creek country on either side of the Walton Road supported several fine communities. (See account of Pleasant Grove Church.)

The Goodpastures, Arnolds, Hinds, Copelands and others came from Overton county, the Martins, Dentons, Wilhites, Lansdens and others were from White county, while many prominent families in Jackson, Smith and De Kalb sent representatives to the new county of Putnam long after pioneer days.

A HISTORY OF PUTNAM COUNTY

CHAPTER TWO

OLD LANDMARKS AND EVENTS

BUCK'S COLLEGE—Less than half a mile east of the corporate limits of Cookeville, on the farm now owned by Dr. J. P. Terry, stands a dilapidated two-story frame structure which for more than seventy years has been known locally as "Buck's College." The greater part of this historic building has been torn away, but enough remains to assure us that it was a large and imposing house in its day. It was here that Isaac Buck and his son, Jonathan, established Andrews College in the early fifties, a successful school of higher education which was at its zenith when the Civil War broke out. When the new county of Putnam was established a strong effort was made to locate the county town around this school, and for a time the prospects were very bright for the proposed "Monticello," but it was finally decided to locate the future metropolis of the mountains upon its present site and with its present name. The details of this contest are given elsewhere.

While this ambitious undertaking was doomed to failure it is a splendid tribute to the worthy men who sought to do big things. The State thought enough of the enterprise to vote financial aid to it—the first instance in its history, so far as we have been able to ascertain.

A brief description of this old structure might be of interest. In shape it somewhat resembled the letter H. The walls were made chiefly of huge poplar logs, nicely hewn and fitted together, and over these a heavy weather-boarding. There were five very large limestone chimneys, with fireplaces up stairs and down. The connecting link between the two main structures was a single room about thirty by sixty feet, which was designed as a dining hall for boarding students. None of the other rooms were under twenty-five feet square, and several exceeded this size. The building was never quite finished and never painted. The first term opened in 1852 and the school was closed soon after the beginning of the Civil War. No attempt was made to revive the institution after the war, although several private schools were conducted in the building. Jonathan Buck, who made it his residence, also taught a private school upstairs for some five or six years, until his health failed. He died in 1885. A man of ripe scholarship, Mr. Buck left a large and valuable library which, unfortunately, was dispersed after his death. He was editor, teacher, photographer and expert penman. This last accomplishment gave him many hours of congenial, but not very remunerative, employment. Neighbors and friends for miles around appealed to him for assistance in drawing up deeds, wills and contracts. Lovesick swains came to exchange farm labor for letters, and such missives as Mr. Buck could compose and set down in his beautiful script must have been very compelling in those days when a letter was a letter.

STANDING STONE—Perhaps the most widely known object of prehistoric interest in this county is the remains of a monolith, originally standing just west of the town of Monterey, near the edge of the plateau. Early travelers over the Walton Road knew it only as the "Standing Stone." Years after it was overturned, rolled some distance and utilized as a "horse-block"—but still the post office for the scattered neighborhood was known as Standing Stone, until Monterey was established. It is current tradition that nothing was inscribed on the rock and that only a few charcoals were found beneath it. In 1897 the Cookeville Lodge of the

A HISTORY OF PUTNAM COUNTY

Independent Order of Red Men, a fraternal organization, removed this stone with impressive public ceremony to a lot in the eastern suburbs of Monterey and placed it permanently upon a massive and elaborate pedestal, where it may be seen from the windows of a passing train. Robert T. Daniel, Grand Incohonee, the national head of the order, was present and delivered an address.

Living in Monterey today is an interesting old couple, Joseph and Fannie Hall, from whose conversation we have gathered many interesting facts. Having spent their long lives upon the plateau they are familiar with its early history and traditions. Speaking of the Standing Stone, Mrs. Hall relates this hitherto unpublished circumstance: "My mother, Mrs. Susan Goodwin, often talked to me about the dangerous trip made across this mountain by her uncle and brother long before any settlement had been made here. They had gone to the Bean camp on the Watauga River to join other movers who were going west with a guard of soldiers. They arrived too late and decided to strike out alone. They made it through safely, thanks to good luck. Among other things they told her of the Standing Stone image at the western edge of the flat land, describing it as a big gray dog in a sitting position, head and ears up, looking straight out west. The fore legs were carved out of the stone. Nearly everybody that passed broke off a little piece to carry away with them."

This last statement is significant and not difficult to believe, knowing what we do of the almost universal vice of vandalism.

If these clear-sighted and cool-headed men of the wilderness saw straight and true—and we have no reason to doubt their veracity—this sphinx-like sculpture may have belonged to a cultured people long antedating the wild and roaming

Indian. Here certainly is a difficult problem for the archaeologist.

STANDING STONE SCHOOLHOUSE—Just about one hundred years ago the hardy pioneers who had settled within five or six miles of that well-known landmark, Standing Stone, remembering the churches and schoolhouses they had left behind them in other states, met and erected what was probably the first public building in the eastern end of the county. It stood on the lot now occupied by the residence of Millard Sehon, in the town of Monterey, and was, of course, made of logs, with "puncheon" floor and split log seats, with board roof held down by log weights. No nails or glass were used. It was pitifully small, only some 16 by 18 feet, but it sufficed to hold the handfull of pioneer children who trudged in for miles around to imbibe learning under the guidance of various itinerant teachers, who conducted subscription schools at intervals. On certain Sundays the entire population gathered in to hear the Methodist "circuit rider"—then a highly appropriate name—preach the gospel. This was their community center and the only place for public meeting for miles around. Among the early teachers who taught there were Jimmie J. Brown, Sims Ely, Irene Ely, Louis Adkins, B. Swift, Robert Simpson, George Walker, Josiah French, Isaac Truitt and Dave Hostler. Prominent among the occasional preachers were Nathan Judd, Isaac Buck and Samuel Lyles, who always preached to crowded houses.

THE BOOGER SWAMP—About one mile and a half east of Cookeville the Buck Mountain Road is crossed by the old Sparta-Livingston Road. Turning to the left here and going about a quarter of a mile in the direction of Livingston one reaches the scene of the noted ante-bellum mystery. The

A HISTORY OF PUTNAM COUNTY

large and dismal swamp that once covered several acres on either side of the road is now only a memory, due to the propensity of modern man to clear, drain and cultivate the soil. But the name, "Booger Swamp," still clings to the spot after nearly three-quarters of a century. One dark night in the early fifties a well-known minister of the gospel, whose name is not essential to our story, was passing this lonely spot on horseback, when suddenly an apparition appeared before him—or, at least, he said it did. After a great deal of discussion and several futile efforts to induce the spook-seeing brother to retract his story, he was finally arraigned in a formal church court and tried, convicted and expelled from the ministry. According to his story, the apparition was a pure white body floating about a yard above the ground and "about the size and length of a weaver's beam," to use his exact language. It made some effort to communicate with him, but his horse became unruly and dashed away.

This was back in the days of slavery, and it is needless to add that no darky would have passed this spot at night for the price of his liberty. But there is no color line in superstition, and many white people of that day—and since—have speeded up a bit when passing through "Booger Swamp."

THE WALTON ROAD—The first Legislature of the State, in the year 1797, authorized Capt. William Walton, a pioneer citizen of Smith County, to construct a more direct route from East Tennessee to Nashville, over which goods and emigrants might be transported. Beginning near the junction of the Tennessee, Clinch and Emory rivers, (the vicinity of Kingston), the new road was located and cut out, rather than constructed, to its terminus at the junction of the Cumberland and Caney Fork rivers. By the use of this road, many miles of overland travel between Knoxville and Nashville could be saved since heavy goods especially could be floated on the Tennessee to Kingston, then transported on wagons to Carthage, a three days journey, then floated down the Cumberland. Moses Fiske, an eminent scholar of his day, surveyed the road.

Capt. William Walton, who is credited with being the first settler at Carthage, where he is buried, was prominent in the early history of Smith County. The minutes of the first meetings of the "Court of Quarterly Sessions and Pleas," in 1799, reveals that he was a man of considerable wealth, a large slaveholder, and a leader among men. In March, 1800, he was appointed "overseer" of the new road from the mouth of Caney Fork (Walton's Ferry) to the head of Snow Creek—a part of the Walton Road. He is mentioned in the court records in connection with other roads in Smith County.

Garrett and Goodpasture's "History of Tennessee," page 255, says: "Early in its history the state had encouraged the investment of individual capital and enterprise in opening and clearing out public roads from one important settlement to another. Such, for instance, was the old Walton Road, extending from South West Point, on the Clinch river, through the Indian reservation called the Wilderness, to the Cumberland river, at the mouth of Caney Fork, where Carthage now stands. In order to encourage an association of citizens to open and keep this road in repair, the Legislature, in 1801, required the Governor to incorporate them under the style of the Cumberland Turnpike Company, with authority to collect tolls from the traveling public. This was the first charter of incorporation for individual profit granted by the state."

The General Assembly of North Carolina made provision

A HISTORY OF PUTNAM COUNTY

in 1787 for a new road to be opened from Campbell's Station in Knox County to Nashville. The road was opened on September 25, 1788. Speaking of this road, Heiskell, in his "History of Andrew Jackson and Early Tennessee Times," makes this rather surprising statement: "The road from Campbell's Station ran through Roane County to South West Point, now Kingston, Tennessee, and the route of the road to Nashville was largely along the line of the present Tennessee Central Railroad, touching well known points as Kingston, Post Oak Springs, Crab Orchard, Crossville, Lebanon, Nashville."

A careful examination of early authorities leads us to doubt the statement that the present site of Lebanon was touched by a through wagon road as early as 1788. The main highway in that part of the state appears to have been north of the Cumberland river and was the popular route as late as 1796. In that year, Rev. Green Hill and others made a trip from North Carolina to Nashville and return, and it appears from his diary that they traveled through Sumner County. McFerrin's "Methodism in Tennessee," Vol. 1, page 308, quotes Hill as follows, speaking of his return trip: "We crossed the Cumberland river at Walton's Ferry, at the mouth of the Caney Fork, and went the new road up the ridge between the Cumberland and the Caney Fork." This "new" road evidently was one of the trails used by horseback travelers just before the construction of the Walton Road, two years later.

Cisco, in his "Historic Sumner County," page 304, falls into an even more unaccountable error when he places Lebanon on the Walton Road! He says: "Capt. Walton inaugurated the plan and was the contractor who built what is known as Walton's Road which connected the Cumberland country with Knoxville and East Tennessee, and was for

A HISTORY OF PUTNAM COUNTY

many years one of the most traveled roads in the state. The construction of the road was a great achievement at that day. The Tennessee Central Railway closely follows its course from Lebanon to Kingston, across the Cumberland mountains."

A reference to Fort Blount, Jackson County, in the Tennessee Historical Magazine, January, 1920, seems to definitely locate the road of 1787-8 north of the Cumberland river. It reads as follows: "A stream of emigration of pioneers flowed northwestwardly through the county of Cumberland to the old Wilderness Road and along this road through Overton and Jackson Counties. Fort Blount stood on the northern bank of the Cumberland river, in Jackson County, on the old Wilderness Road leading to the settlement at Nashville. It was established in 1794 for the protection of travelers against the Indians, who disputed the right of the white people to use this thoroughfare without compensation to them. The route from Fort Blount to Nashville was the old road begun in 1787. It ran westwardly through Jackson County, the northern part of Smith County, the present county of Trousdale, Sumner County, past the site of Gallatin, then followed closely the present Nashville and Gallatin turnpike to Nashville."

A further confirmation of the popularity of this route as late as 1796 is contained in a foot note in the Tennessee Historical Magazine, October, 1919: "The route then traveled from Knoxville to Nashville was the old road, which began at Leas Springs in Grainger County and ran through the present counties of Knox, Roane, Morgan, Fentress, Overton, Jackson, Smith, Trousdale, Sumner and Davidson. It was opened by the militia in 1787. The Walton Road, which ran mainly through the tier of counties just southward, was opened about 1799."

A HISTORY OF PUTNAM COUNTY

In the "Life of Jefferson Dillard Goodpasture," by A. V. and W. H. Goodpasture, we find this interesting sketch: "There had long been a trace across the mountain from South West Point to the Cumberland settlements. Francis Baily traveled it in 1796, and has left an interesting account of his journey. But at the time the Goodpastures crossed the mountains a wagon road had been recently marked out, under the authority of the General Assembly, between South West Point and the mouth of the Caney Fork river, where Carthage was afterwards established. The work was the enterprise of Capt. William Walton (1760-1816), a native of Bertie County, North Carolina, who had enlisted at the age of seventeen as a private in the Revolutionary War, and served till its close in 1783, coming out with the rank of Captain. He emigrated to the Cumberland settlement in 1785, and located his military land warrant on the north bank of the Cumberland river, at its confluence with the Caney Fork, in 1786. The road, which still bears his name, was about a hundred miles in length, and contained four stands for the accommodation of travelers. Coming west, the first of these was at Kimbroughs, on the eastern foot of the mountain; the second at Crab Orchard, a once famous place on the mountain plateau in Cumberland County; the third at White Plains, in Putnam County, on the western foot of the mountain; and the fourth, near Pekin, also in Putnam County. The road was completed in 1801. In the fall of 1802, Michaux writes of this road: 'The road that crosses this part of the Indian territory, cuts through the mountain in Cumberland; it is as broad and commodious as those in the environs of Philadelphia, in consequence of the amazing number of emigrants that travel through it to go and settle in the Western Country. It is, notwithstanding, in some places, very rugged, but nothing near so much as the one that leads from Stratsburg to Bedford in Pennsylvania. About forty miles from Nashville we met an emigrant in a carriage, followed by their slaves on foot, that had performed their journey without accident. Little boards, painted black and nailed upon the trees, indicate to travelers the distance they have to go.'"

In the year 1800, when the Goodpastures crossed the Wilderness the road was neither so good nor so safe as when Michaux traveled it, although even then, it was not considered prudent to travel it except in parties, on account of roving bands of Indians, one of which he met before he reached South West Point.

F. A. Michaux, the eminent French naturalist, made a tour of scientific investigation through this country in 1803, and his observations, quoted above, indicate that the Walton Road was no mean thoroughfare in its early days. Moses Fiske was his traveling companion.

Moses Fiske, the surveyor of the Walton Road, was born in Massachusetts in 1759, coming to Tennessee in 1796. He first settled at Knoxville but later lived in Davidson, Sumner and Smith counties. In 1805 he laid off the town of Hilham, in Overton County, where he established the Fisk Female Academy, by legislative authority. The Tennessee Historical Magazine says of him that "He was scholarly and he carried on an extensive correspondence with historical and antiquarian societies."

Putnam County has more miles of the Walton Road than has any other county through which it passes. Beginning at the Cumberland County line, the railroad very nearly parallels it on through Monterey and Bilbrey to the vicinity of Brotherton. Here the railroad works around to the north to find gradual descent from the first bench of the mountain by way of Paragon, while the Walton Road, running a little south, proceeds to a rather precipitous descent at Buck Mountain. The railroad and the old highway are again in close proximity near the fairgrounds, north of Cookeville, and do not deviate more than a mile at any point until they reach Baxter. Here the railroad is about one mile on the south and continues its divergence, while the Walton Road runs slightly nort of west in the general direction of Ensor, Gentry and Chestnut Mound, following the main ridges to reduce grades, to its terminus at the old Walton's Ferry, at Carthage.

THE BRASWELL HANGING—Perhaps the largest crowd that was ever assembled in Putnam County, variously estimated by old citizens at from ten to fifteen thousand people, was in Cookeville on the 27th day of March, 1878, to witness the public execution of Teke and Joe Braswell, brothers, convicted of the murder of Russ Allison more than three years previously. This shocking crime occurred at the Allison place, a well-known stand on the Walton Road, about one mile from Baxter, on the night of Nov. 29th, 1875. Dop Johnson and Doll Bates were along, and the latter was sentenced to twenty-one years in the penitentiary. Johnson made a full confession and escaped prosecution. It is not our purpose, after fifty years, to parade the harrowing details of this foul crime, neither would we reopen the question of the guilt or innocense of the accused, but in the interest of historical accuracy we must at least make passing mention of this conspicuous event—the first and only legal execution ever carried out in our county.

THE GUNTER TRAGEDY—A deplorable tragedy of Civil War times that has been invested with a fiction or romance not warranted by the facts, was the slaying of two men

A HISTORY OF PUTNAM COUNTY

and the serious wounding a third by a young girl, Marina Gunter, daughter of John Gunter, one night in March, 1865. This bloody episode has been rather widely exploited as the outcome of political feeling—a tottering old Confedarate sympathizer being whipped by Yankee soldiers, when his daughter rushed to the rescue. The truth of the matter is, the question of politics was not even remotely involved, since all of the parties concerned were republicans and unionists.

The facts here set out were given to the writer by several of the best citizens of Baxter, near the scene of the tragedy Old Sam Patton and John Gunter had swapped horses, and the latter, claiming that he had been cheated, was preparing to bring suit against Patton for damages. Thinking to head this off, Patton induced his son, Tom, and a nephew, Alvin Maxwell, and B. F. Miller, to go over to Gunter's, call the old man out and give a whipping with some advice about leaving the country—not an uncommon proceeding in that day.

The three boys, with courage stimulated by drink, proceeded to carry out instructions. Patton held the horses, while Maxwell and Miller called old man Gunter to the gate and then forced him to accompany them to a spot about a hundred yards from his house and were applying the whip, when a son and daughter in the house, hearing their father's cries, rushed to his aid. Marina, the heroine, armed with a keen-edged axe led the way. Passing Patton with the horses, she slashed at him, nearly severing his arm. Next she fell upon Maxwell and Miller with all of the fury and superhuman strength of one possessed, chopping them with the axe until they fell. The two desperately wounded young men were found next day in a large hollow stump where they had been placed, presumably, by the

Gunters. They were carried to the house of a Mr. Presley, not far away, where Maxwell lived nine days and Miller eighteen days. Patton's wound healed in the usual length of time. Marina Gunter, high-strung and impulsive, was perhaps justifiable from her point of view and understanding. She lived to a ripe old age, passing away only a short time ago. Sam Gunter, the sole survivor, still lives near Baxter.

THE BATTLE OF DUG HILL—The nearest approach to a battle ever staged upon the soil of Putnam County was the short but sanguinary engagement at Dug Hill, on the Calf Killer, during the Civil War. A company of Federal cavalry led by Capt. Exum was returning from a little raid up the Calf Killer to their base at Sparta. The Confederates, under Capt. Hughes, anticipating their return, had arranged an ambuscade at Dug Hill, where the road winds around the mountain—an ideal spot for a surprise attack. The Confederate infantry, scattered along above the road behind logs and trees, Indian fashion, suddenly opened fire upon the massed body of unsuspecting cavalrymen. There was a wild stampede of blue-coats and many empty saddles, and the survivors were moved by unanimous desire to quit the scene immediately—which they did, closely pursued by the invisible foe. The casualties in this one-sided action totaled about sixty, practically all on the Federal side. About 180 men were engaged in the fight, equally divided between the opposing armies.

THE SIEGE AT WATERLOO.—This episode, known generally as the "Peek Fight," came very near a tragic ending, and but for the timely intervention of cool-headed citizens ten of Uncle Sam's picked "raiders" would have raided no more. Back in 1880 illicit distilling had become so open and notorious in the section known locally as "Little Putnam," that the revenue officers were instructed to clean it out. Joe Spurrier, a fearless and efficient raider, led a body of selected men into this paradise of moonshiners. The well organized "shiners" quickly mobilized about fifty armed men who surrounded the "revenues," forcing them to take refuge in a nearby house, which happened to be the residence of Benjamin Loftis. Here they were besieged for three days without food or water and were constantly under fire. Maj. J. C. Freeze, Elijah Terry and perhaps others, went among the moonshiners and persuaded them to allow the revenue officers to depart in peace. The besiegers had decided to burn the house and slaughter the hated raiders, and it was with great difficulty that they were restrained.

THE ROLLEN PLACE.—Years before the Civil War, just how many we cannot say, "Baldy" Rollen kept an inn for the accommodation of travelers on the Walton Road, about 2½ miles above Gentry. Rollen's reputation seems to have been very bad and for years it was whispered in the neighborhood that often travelers stopping with him for the night were never seen to continue their journey. However that may be, he felt the heavy hand of the law in his old age. It is said that one day a woman and two children, traveling alone, stopped at the Rollen inn and asked for something to eat. She was brutally murdered with an axe, but the children were allowed to escape. Rollen was tried and convicted and sent to the penitentiary, where he spent his last years. The old house has long since disappeared and no descendants of the name remain, but old settlers still point out a large tree by the road side, under which it is alleged the crime was committed.

A HISTORY OF PUTNAM COUNTY

CLATORS'S PLACE—The earliest place of amusement to be set up in the county as a business venture was a Bowling Alley on the corner of the north side of the Square and Washington Avenue, in Cookeville. About the year 1874 a man named Clator dropped into town, secured a lot and proceeded to erect an ornate and really attractive place of amusement. Of course it contained a bar, but we had had saloons before, several of them, and that was nothing new. But the Alley was a decided success—for awhile. Mr. Clator was an accomplished banjo-picker and every public day in town his place was crowded. Norman Shaw, son of Joseph Shaw, was his understudy and apt pupil, and soon he was rated almost as good as his teacher. Clator's palace of amusement lasted only about three years, but long after his departure Norman Shaw continued to perform brilliantly on his banjo for the free entertainment of many delighted auditors, who felt that no public day in Cookeville was quite complete until they had heard Norman play.

THE STAGE ROBBERY.—One day in the year 1881, as the old Nashville stage coach came lumbering down the Walton Road in the vicinity of Pond Spring (Pekin), three masked men stepped from a clump of bushes on the road side, and ordered Uncle John Reyburn, the veteran driver, to hold up his hands. The outlaws were "Bug" Hunt and two Edwards boys. After securing several hundred dollars from the passengers they disappeared in the woods. Miss Z. Martin, Cookeville, was enroute to Nashville, but the robbers courteously refrained from taking her valuables. A runner was at once dispatched to Cookeville, and that night Sheriff Henry J. Brown with a posse started in hot but fruitless pursuit. A few days later Hunt was arrested by Jeff Lee, Bob Maddux and David Haynes. He was tried, convicted and sentenced to the penitentiary for a term of years. After serving his time he reformed and, we are told, is still living a respectable life. The Edwards boys escaped and were never apprehended.

INTERVIEWS WITH OLD CITIZENS:—Mr. Calvin Crook, 94, who has known this region from boyhood, relates interesting stories told him by his mother of the many six-horse wagons that used to pass through the country when she was a girl, going north and south, with freight of all kinds, and how they would often stall on the steep unworked hills. Most of the north-bound wagons were laden with cotton from Georgia and Alabama for the mills of the north.

Speaking of the location of the town of Cookeville, Mr. Crook says that his uncle, Charles Crook, was naturally very anxious for the town to be built upon his land, and since running water was deemed essential, the "big spring" near the center of his property was his chief talking point, and he made the most of it. However, the partisans of a rival site spread the report that Crook's spring was in the habit of going dry! Interested parties met at the spring on one occasion to determine the truth of this report. One witness stated that on a certain occasion he had visited the spring and found it bone dry and a dead fox in it. This was too much for Mr. Crook, who jumped up and cried out, "No, it was not a fox; it was that hoe you stole from me!" And so with much bad feeling and no little juggling and lobbying the site was finally decided upon.

Mr. Crook tells us that Jesse Crook, another uncle, swapped a pony worth about $40 or $50 for two hundred acres of land, which he afterwards sold to Charles Crook

A HISTORY OF PUTNAM COUNTY

for $100. A few months later Charles sold forty acres of this land to the Chairman of the Putnam county court for $100. So everybody made a little money in these various transactions—and still Putnam county got her town site cheap enough after all. In this connection, we might state that the Public Square was laid off on the eastern side of this tract, not in the center. The land of George and James Ramsey came with a block of the Square and was later purchased by James M. Douglass and Stephen D. Burton, who divided it, Douglass taking the part south of the Buck Mountain Road and Burton the part north of it.

Jacob E. Matheny, of Munday, Texas, tells us: "In the year 1844 my father came across the Cumberland Mountain over the Walton Road. When he reached the Joe Allison place he turned back as far as Double Springs, where he took the Gainesboro road and went seven miles to the old Fort Blount road. He bought land about a mile from the Basham place, and two miles from John Cummins' mill. Wylie Knight, who lived on Knight's Creek, was the oldest citizen. He was a Deputy Sheriff of Jackson county, and claimed to have come to this section before Tennessee was originated. My father got his mail at White Plains (Southeast of Algood) at the store of Stephen D. Burton. The spot where Cookeville now is was covered with oak bushes and chinqueapin. It was a fine cattle range and many deer lived in it. When the county line was run between Jackson and Putnam I was with the surveyors two days, from Mount Union church, eight miles north of Cookeville, to an old church house on the Sparta road, two miles from where Bloomington now is. Levi Whitefield taught a little school there about the year 1855. Mathew Kuykendall and Ridley Draper owned land around Bloomington, and in 1857, Garland Kuykendall built up a good school there which he conducted until 1861. Richard Cooke owned a very large tract of land south of Bloomington, known at that time as the "Big Woods."

"Richard Brooks represented Jackson county in the Legislature before Putnam was established. He stayed at my father's house when canvassing this part of the county and I traveled with him several days. We went to one place where we expected to get dinner, but the man was not at home and his wife did not know us. Brooks asked a small boy who was standing in the door what his name was. The woman spoke up quickly, 'Tell the man you are named after that double-headed devil Dick Brooks,' whereupon Brooks ran his hand down in his home-made jeans and brought out a dollar which he handed to the boy. Then we departed without any dinner.

"Returning from the war in 1865, I went to work in store of J. M. Douglass. Anderson Sloan and J. C. Freeze were also selling goods here then. The same year a company of Federal soldiers was sent from Nashville to keep the peace, but that did not work so well and they soon fell back. That was my last experience with soldiers. Three well known men in Cookeville about that time were Lige Carr, Tom Jerry Bradford and Fen Laycock. They were always present.

"When I was a boy we only knew of one doctor—Dr. Fane. Later we had Goodpasture, Baker, McClain, Martin, Dyer, Robinson, and others.

"Not only did the early settlers wear home-spun cloth, but men's hats were also manufactured to order. Within three miles of Cookeville, Messrs. Paul, Hamilton and Phillips were noted for the fine hats they could turn out.

A HISTORY OF PUTNAM COUNTY

Nathan Judd, a Mr. Bullock and J. R. Hancock were expert tanners of all kinds of leather.

"The year 1855 was the 'dry year,' in Jackson and many people went to the rich hill country in Putnam for corn."

John T. Askew, eighty-five years old, widely known and highly respected, gave us this interview: "I was born on Wilkin's Creek, Dekalb county, July 9, 1840, and located at Buffalo Valley, Putnam county, Jan. 1, 1867, where I have since resided. The old log school and church house, about a mile up the Valley, was our only public meeting place. Capt. Exum, who was the first merchant here, boarded at my house. Samuel Young was considered the richest man in the county. When I came to the Valley the well known citizens in this section were, as well as I remember: Snowden Maddux, Joshua Bartlett, Matthew Scudder, Thomas Maddux, Samuel Young, David Nichols, John Evans, Peter Young, Jonathan Denny, Timothy Denny, Robert Alcorn, James Isbell, Jenkins Jones, Loona Thompson, George Maddux, John Jared, Bradley Maddux. Perhaps I have forgotten some. Soon after the war Green Duke, the founder of a religious sect called the 'Dukeites,' gained a considerable following here. He claimed that he could handle snakes and drink poisons and that he would never die. After his death the sect died out. The first time I was in Cookeville I was about sixteen years old and went there with my father to a horse race. We had been to a big race at Smithville and went on to Cookeville, passing through Mine Lick. In those days there were numerous race tracks in this and adjoining counties, plenty of whiskey and lots of gambling. These were good places for gamblers to meet and try their luck."

A HISTORY OF PUTNAM COUNTY

CHAPTER THREE

PUTNAM COUNTY FORMED

At the time that Tennessee was admitted into the Union, most of the wilderness, now known as the Upper Cumberland country, was a part of Sumner County, becoming a part of the new county of Smith in 1799, and a part of Jackson County in 1801. Overton and White were both established in 1806, and then county building ceased in this section of the State for many years.

The Acts of the Tennessee Legislature of the year 1801, Chapter 48, reads as follows:

"Be it enacted, That a new county be established by the name of Jackson; That the Quarterly Courts of Jackson County be held on the second Monday in December, March, June and September, at the house of John Bowen, on Roaring River, with the same powers as other courts, heretofore established by law; That, Charles Cavanaugh, Esq., William Sullivan, Sr., Andrew Greer, Thomas Smith, Sr., and Thomas Draper, be, and they are hereby appointed, Commissioners, who, or a majority of them, shall have full power and authority to purchase forty acres of land, to build a Courthouse, Prison and Stocks, as near the center of the county as the situation will admit, to be called by the name of Smithfield, etc." In detail it is set forth how these Commissioners were to be sworn or affirm to do equal and impartial justice to the people, sell lots, build a Courthouse, Prison and Stocks, and were required to give bond in the sum of $5,000, and when their work was completed to lay an account of all cost before the Court, at least five members or a majority of the J. P's. to be present before any allowance could be made. The Act pro-

A HISTORY OF PUTNAM COUNTY

vides further that all elections for members of the General Assembly, the Governor, and members of Congress, shall be held at the Courthouse in Jackson County, and that the Sheriff of Jackson County shall meet the Sheriff of Sumner County at the Courthouse in said county, on the succeeding Monday, to examine the respective polls, or votes, cast, and declare the persons duly elected and give certificates of election. This act was passed November 6, 1801. The use of "Stocks" as a method of punishment carries us back to colonial days.

On November 14, 1801, this additional act was passed: "Be it Enacted by the General Assembly of the State of Tennessee that the bounds of Jackson County shall be as follows: Beginning at the Northeast corner of said county on the State line, thence east with said line to the Northwest corner of Anderson County, thence along the Western boundary of the counties of Anderson and Roane to the Southern boundary of the State, thence westward with said line to a point from which a due north line will strike the southeast corner of said county."

Out of this vast territory many new counties have been formed.

As population increased, the need for the establishment of the new county became imperative. Responding to this agitation, the State Legislature, in February, 1842, passed a bill entitled, "An Act to Establish the County of Putnam, to perpetuate the name and public services of General Israel Putnam, of the Revolutionary War." The territory was to be taken from the counties of Jackson, Overton, White and Fentress. White Plains was named as the place where all courts should be held, until a permanent site could be established for the new county. This was the farm of S. D. Burton, 3½ miles east of Cookeville. The

A HISTORY OF PUTNAM COUNTY

Commissioners appointed to carry out the Act were: Issac Buck, Burton Marchbanks, H. D. Marchbanks, Richard F. Cooke, Henry L. McDaniel, Carr Terry, Elijah Carr, Lawson Clark and Grover Maddux. The Act provided that Mounce Gore, a well-known surveyor of Jackson County, should survey and make a plot of the new county site. It further provided that as soon as the Commissioners should decide upon the location of the county site they should make a report to the County Court, which would appoint five Commissioners, "who shall proceed to lay off a town at the point designated to be known by the name of Monticello, with as many streets and such width as they may deem necessary, reserving at least three acres for a Public Square, a lot for a jail and lots for a male and female Academy and for a Church for public worship." The Commissioners were duly empowered to sell lots in the proposed new town of Monticello, and with the proceeds establish a fund to be used in the purchase of land and the erection of public buildings. The members of the Commission were: James Bartlett, William H. Vance, John Bohannon, Edward Anderson and James Jackson. After a long delay the Commissioners finally, in 1844, decided upon a location about a mile east of the present town of Cookeville—the Buck College site—but their plans never matured. The same year a suit was instituted in the Chancery Court of Overton County seeking to enjoin William H. Carr, Clerk of the Circuit Court, and Joseph A. Ray, Clerk of the County Court, from the exercise of their official duties. The Court sustained this contention and held that the new county of Putnam had been illegally and unconstitutionally established. This chaotic condition existed for some ten years.

When the General Assembly of the State met in 1854,

A HISTORY OF PUTNAM COUNTY

a petition was presented asking for the re-establishment of the county of Putnam, the Supreme Court having decided in a similar case that once duly organized a county could not be enjoined in the performance of its functions. An Act was then passed making some slight changes in the boundary lines and providing that court should be held at the house of Lewis Huddleston, "near Salem meeting house and camping ground," until a permanent site could be located and a courthouse erected. It was provided that the new town should be named "Cookeville," in honor of Maj. Richard F. Cooke, a prominent and public-spirited citizen who lived in the vicinity of what is now Double Springs, on a plantation of several thousand acres. Maj. Cooke had been very active in the movement to secure a new county, and it was generally conceded that it was a just and fitting compliment to give his name to the new town.

Acts of 1852, Chapter 320:

An act to re-establish the county of Putnam. Passed Feb. 11.

"Whereas, an act of the General Assembly, passed on the 1st of February, 1842, entitled, 'An act to establish the county of Putnam, to perpetuate the name of General Israel Putnam of the Revolutionary War,' Chapter 179, and under the operation of said act and other acts subsequent thereto, the county was completely organized by the election of all the proper officers, both civil and military, and by holding of Circuit and County Courts, at the time established by law. This state of things continued until the spring of 1844; and a bill in equity and for an injunction was filed in the Chancery Court of Overton County against William H. Carr, Clerk of the Circuit Court, and Joseph A. Ray, Clerk of the County Court, and other officers in Putnam County enjoining them from further acting in their official capacity; and no answer or demurrer or plea being put in, the bill was taken for confessed and the said injunction was rendered perpetual, and the said County was declared by the Court of Chancery not to have been legally and constitutionally established, and the functions of all officers have ceased since that period. And

"Whereas, the Supreme Court of this state has decided in the case of Ford vs. Farmer, et als, 8th Humphreys, page 152, that after the organization of a county is complete, and the original Commissioners have executed their duty, that it is not the province or within the jurisdiction of the courts of justice to enjoin the civil officers of a county from proceeding in their official duties; and therefore, the decree of the Court of Chancery rendered in the case above specified was and is not binding, except as to the parties on record; and it is represented to this Legislature, by petition and otherwise, that the Constitution has not been violated by the establishment of the County of Putnam, and the citizens residing within the limits of said county are desirous that the county may be re-established, therefore,

"SEC. 1—Be it enacted, etc., That the said county of Putnam is hereby re-established, with all of the powers and privileges of other counties, of the State of Tennessee and with all the butts, bounds and lines that governed the limits of said county at the time said bill of injunction was filed against the officers of said county, except such as may hereinafter be provided for in this act.

"SEC. 2—That the bounds of said county of Putnam shall be as originally run by Mounce Gore, principal surveyor, and his deputies, with such alterations as may be necessary to preserve the constitutionality of said county, or better promote the interests of her citizens; *Provided*,

A HISTORY OF PUTNAM COUNTY

that in no case the change of any of the original lines shall affect the constitutional right of the old counties, and the beginning corner shall be on the south bank of the Cumberland River where the line dividing Smith and Jackson Counties crosses said river, running up said river with its various meanders to the mouth of Indian Creek; thence in a south-east direction with Mounce Gore's last line, upon the extreme height of the dividing ridge, to a point from which an east line crosses Martin's Creek, near the mouth Shaw's Branch; thence in an eastern direction with said Gore's line as last run, crossing the road leading from Sparta to Gainesboro, between the twelve and thirteen mile posts at about twelve and a half miles from Gainesboro; thence with said Gore's line through Jackson County to the west boundary line of Overton County, to the original corners of Putnam County on said line; thence with said Gore's last line through Overton County, bearing twelve miles south of Livingston to George McCormick's old stand in Fentress County, on the road leading from Brady's turnpike gate to Jamestown; thence with the original line of Putnam County in the direction of Morgan County line as far as two miles, if necessary, to preserve the constitutional limits in territory to the said County of Putnam; thence in a southeastern direction, so as to strike the Morgan County line north of Johnson's Stand on Walton's Road, at or near the same distance that it may be necessary to run east of George McCormick's; thence with said Morgan County line south to said Johnson's Stand on Walton's Road; thence south two degrees west five miles to the southeast corner of said County, marked P. C.; thence west five miles with said original line to the declivity of the Cumberland Mountains; thence with John Welch's last line through White County, leaving the town of Sparta at

A HISTORY OF PUTNAM COUNTY

the distance of twelve miles, to the mouth of Hutchin's Creek; thence down the Falling Water with its various meanders to the east boundary line of DeKalb County where said line crosses Falling Water near the falls; thence in a southern direction, crossing said river with said DeKalb county line one and a half miles; thence in a north western direction, crossing said Falling Water between the mouth of Cane Creek and Riley Medley's old place on said river, and crossing Mine Lick Creek twelve miles from the town of Smithville in DeKalb County; and thence in a western direction bearing twelve miles north of Smithville to the Jackson County line; thence west with the north boundary line of DeKalb County to the Caney Fork River; thence down said river with its various meanders to the mouth of Rock Spring Creek in Smith County; and thence in a northern direction to a point in the line dividing Smith and Jackson Counties south of Walton's Road and opposite the upper end of Major James McDaniel's farm, thence north crossing the Walton's Road with said Jackson County line to the beginning."

For half a century previous to the erection of Putnam County, its territory was largely included in the bounds of White, Jackson and Overton—the three counties cornering on a large chestnut tree, on the north side of the Walton Road, at White Plains.

The newly re-organized county of Putnam started off with the following officials: Pleas Bohannon, Sheriff; Curtis Mills, Circuit Court Clerk; Russell Moore, County Court Clerk; Dr. William Baker, Register; Joe Pierson, Tax Collector; W. Gentry, Trustee; R. D. Allison, Chairman of the County Court.

Many new families moved in from surrounding counties and business of all kinds seemed prosperous. Several new

A HISTORY OF PUTNAM COUNTY

enterprises were projected, real estate took on new values. Professional men came to grow up with the new town. Harvey H. Dillard, young attorney, hung out his shingle in 1855, and a year later Holland Denton, another young aspirant, opened his law office.

THE CIVIL WAR—The coming on of the Civil War in 1861 cut short the progress and beclouded the bright prospects of the new county, so recently established. The people of property generally were slave-holders and, with few exceptions, were favorable to secession. Many volunteers rushed to the front at the outbreak of hostilities, few waiting for conscription. Capt. H. H. Dillard, of Cookeville, raised the first company of infantry to go from this county. Others quickly followed. We regret that we have not a complete roster of these brave and patriotic men.

While a few prominent men, mostly Whig in politics, stood resolutely for the Union, thereby incurring the suspicion and enmity of their neighbors, the overwhelming mass of our people were for complete seperation as the best solution. The only Union sentiment of any consequence was in certain restricted areas in the western and south-western parts of the county. In this connection it is interesting to note that of the three Union Generals furnished by Tennessee, one, Gen. A. C. Gillem, was from Putnam County.

Although we cannot now ascertain the exact number of slaves owned in this county at the time of the emancipation, old citizens are agreed that this item of wealth far exceeded all others combined. This sudden and unexpected shrinkage in the volume of property meant financial ruin to our people generally, and when we add to this the burden of four years of non-production, together with the ravages of opposing armies, the devastation assumes heart-breaking proportions. It need occasion no surprise that the recovery was slow and

A HISTORY OF PUTNAM COUNTY

painful; the marvel is that we have done so well. Certain more favored sections of one common country, with a hundred years the start of us and no cataclysmic destruction of property, have surpassed us, it is quite true, in schools and roads and public improvements, but they should have done much better. Our people are not indifferent to these public blessings and conveniences and mean to have them as fast as population and wealth will admit. The point we would stress is that, resources and ability considered, no section of our common country has made more real progress, and this alone justifies the confident expectation of a wonderful future.

Speaking of the Civil War period brings up in memory the names of many worthy leaders of Putnam County, who did their duty gloriously and have since passed to their reward—Captains H. H. Dillard, J. H. Curtis, S. G. Slaughter, Walton Smith, Jackson Davis, John B. Vance, Holland Denton, S. H. McDearman, John S. Quarles, W. B. Carlen, S. J. Johnson, Rison Robinson, William Ensor, Abraham Ford, P. Jones, S. M. McCaleb, Wade Jones, Maj. J. C. Freeze, Col. Sidney S. Stanton and Gen. Alvin Gillem.

Captain H. H. Dillard, who led the first company of volunteers from Putnam County, wrote an extended article for Lindsley's, "Military Annals of Tennessee," page 335, in which he says: "The company I led out, known as the 'Highlanders,' was from Putnam County; organized in May and mustered into service at Camp Trousdale, 9th of June, 1861. It helped to form the Sixteenth Tennessee Infantry, and constituted the extreme left of the regiment, and was lettered as Co. K.: H. H. Dillard, Captain; W. K. Sadler, First Lieutenant; H. Denton, Second Lieutenant and R. A. Young, Third Lieutenant. John H. Savage was elected

Colonel.

Capt. Dillard says, in concluding his article, that due to the reorganization and consolidation of companies he necessarily lost sight of many of his men, but he is convinced that fully three-fourths of those going out with him at the beginning of the war were killed, wounded or died of disease. He adds: "My company—in fact, nearly the whole regiment—was composed of what you might term mountain men. They were healthy and strong; some with more and some with less education—not one in the company, I believe, who did not write his signature to the muster rolls. They were courageous and prompt to duty in camp and upon the field, and not one ever acted the coward in battle."

Capt. Dillard's article, which is too lengthy for reproduction here, begins with an account of the march to Huntersville, Va., about a month after his company had been sworn in, and where they were in camp for about one month, suffering greatly from typhiod and with many deaths. One dark rainy night they were ordered to cook five day's rations and proceed to Valley Mountain. It was on this march that the intrepid Col. Savage got in action. He was in advance of the main body of troops when three pickets were captured, from whom it was learned that an entire company, "Cincinnati Grays," were camped near by. Col. Savage, too impatient to wait for his troops to come up, put spurs to "Old George" and dashed into the midst of the thunderstruck enemy, as green as he was in the art of war, and when he flourished his huge pistols and thundered out, "Throw down your arms or I will have you all shot!" they quickly obeyed. The speedy appearance of his troops saved the doughty Colonel from an embarrassing situation. A few days later the companies of Captains Dillard and York had their first baptism of fire in a sharp engagement with about 300 of the enemy, losing two killed and three wounded. The Federal loss was 13 killed and 17 prisoners. The Confederates were armed with flint-lock muskets.

Cheat Mountain was strongly fortified by the Federals, but Gen. Jackson was too wise and humane to attempt to take it by storm, much to the impatience of his troops. The Sixteenth was next to strengthen the line before which the Federals under Gen. Rosecrans were threatening an attack, but Gen. Lee, realizing his strategic position, held his army on the defensive and later Rosecrans withdrew, just as Lee had foreseen. Winter coming on, the Sixteenth was ordered to Charleston S. C., to do coast guard duty.

In April soon after the battle of Shiloh they were ordered to Corinth and were in the trenches for some time, and later followed Bragg through Kentucky to Perryville, back to Murfreesboro, Chickamauga, Missionary Ridge, Kenesaw Mountain, Rocky Face, Resaca, etc. Then, under Generals Johnson and Hood, successively, Peach Tree Creek, Jonesboro, Franklin, and Nashville, on up to the surrender in North Carolina.

We copy the roster of Captain Dillard's Company from Thomas A. Head's history of the "Sixteenth Regiment:"

OFFICERS
H. H. Dillard, Captain
W. K. Sadler, First Lieutenant
Holland Denton, Second Lieutenant
R. A. Young, Third Lieutenant
M. S. Smith, First Sargeant
S. W. Brown, Second Sargeant
B. F. Scudders, Third Sargeant
James McKinley, Fourth Sargeant
David H. Bullington, Fifth Sargeant
H. I. Hughes, First Corporal
J. M. Null, Second Corporal
Joel Gabbert, Third Corporal

J. Y. Crowell, Fourth Corporal
PRIVATES

M. M. Anderson
F. M. Amonette
Joseph Ballard
C. M. Ballard
Samuel Benson
J. R. Bullington
Leroy Bullington
John Bullington
Josiah Boyd
Obadiah Boyd
J. A. Boyd
John Brown
David Bryant
W. F. Grimsley
Jack Griffin
Elijah Garrett
Noah Harris
Richard Hensley
William Hoggard
Henry Harpole
William Hodges
J. M. Jackson
Alexander Jackson
G. M. Jaquess
P. H. Ledbetter
Thomas Laycock
I. C. Laycock
W. W. Baldwin
William Braswell
W. N. Caruthers
Crockett Clark
D. A. Crowell
Walter E. Chilton
John Choate
Jacob Choate
Meadow Choate
J. L. Davis

G. W. Floyd
J. H. Fisher
W. L. Grimsley
J. J. Ricardson
John Scarlett
B. L. Scarlett
A. J. Sutton
W. H. Sullins
T. C. Thompson
John Tolbert
J. B. Vance
P. M. Wassom
Allen Winchester
William Wiggleton
J. L. Laycock
W. H. Maxwell
D. W. Maxwell
T. R. Matheney
J. P. Mayberry
W. T. Moore
J. F. Moore
J. R. Murray
M. J. Nichols
John H. Nichols
Lewis Ollerson
J. F. Owen
W. H. H. Ortry
H. L. C. Pearson
D. G. Pointer
R. J. West
J. M. West
B. H. Watson
W. W. Wallace
A. D. Young
C. C. Young
R. R. McDaniel
Rufus Owen

A HISTORY OF PUTNAM COUNTY

Van Dillard
I. C. Eldridge

William Webb
Albert Ballard

KILLED

M. M. Anderson, Perryville
John Choate, Murfreesboro
Jacob Choate, Murfreesboro
W. F. Grimsley, Perryville
J. C. Laycock, Murfreesboro
John Brown, Murfreesboro
J. R. Murray, Perryville
J. F. Owen, Jonesboro
Capt. J. B. Vance, Perryville
T. C. Thompson, Perryville
R. J. West, Atlanta
Rufus Owen, Atlanta
William Webb, Franklin

Lieut. W. W. Wallace, Murfreesboro
Joseph Y. Ballard, Murfreesboro
Lieut. D. G. Pointer, Perryville
William Hodges, Chickamauga
Alexander Jackson, Perryville
James Murray, Murfreesboro
Albert Ballard, Murfreesboro

DIED IN SERVICE

W. T. Moore, Dublin, Va.
Bransford Boyd, Nashville (1861)
T. B. Matheney, Huntersville
David H. Bullington, Tupelo
John Tolbert, Millsboro

WOUNDED

R. F. Sudders, Perryville
John Bullington, Perryville
Josiah Bullington, Perryville
John Brown, Perryville
W. W. Baldwin, Perryville
W. N. Caruthers, Perryville
M. J. Nichols, Perryville
Lewis Ollerson, Perryville
W. H. H. Ortry, Atlanta
H. L. C. Pearsons, Perryville
J. J. Richardson, Perryville
I. M. West, Atlanta

H. I. Hodges, Perryville and Murfreesboro
John Nichols, Perryville and Murfreesboro
William Wiggleton, Murfreesboro
J. H. Fisher,, Cheat Mountain
Joseph Ballard, Murfreesboro
P. N. Wassom, Murfreesboro

A HISTORY OF PUTNAM COUNTY

PROMOTED

H. H. Dillard, Major, 1862   F. M. Amonette, Capt., 1863
John B. Vance, Capt., 1862   J. F. Owen, 3rd. Lieut., 1863
W. W. Baldwin, 2nd., Lieut., 1862
W. W. Wallace, 1st., Lieut., 1862
D. C. Pointer, 3rd., Lieut., 1862
M. J. Nichols, 3rd., Lieut., 1863

In the fall of 1862 the Eighth Tennessee Cavalry was organized at Yankeetown, White County, with George D. Dibrell, Colonel. Under his splendid leadership many sons of Putnam County went to the front—so many, in fact, that some of the largest reunions of the famous "Old Eighth Cavalry" were held in Cookeville, notably the one on Nov. 2, 1889. Gen. Dibrell having died at his home in Sparta, May 9, 1888, Hon. George H. Morgan delivered an able and touching address in memory of the departed leader. The Memorial Committee was as follows: George H. Morgan, S. D. Bilbrey, C. J. Davis, J. D. Bartlett, W. R. Hill, Henry P. Davis, W. P. Chapin, J. H. Curtis. We regret that we have space for only a few paragraphs from Mr. Morgan's address. Here is one: "After leaving Gen. Wheeler on his raid into Middle Tennessee in the fall of 1864, Gen. Dibrell did some of the most extraordinary marching and fighting on record. Being separated from Gen. Wheeler, he and Gen. Williams, of Kentucky, passed with their brigades up the mountain east of Cookeville, on across through Wartburg and thence to Bristol, then to Saltville, Virginia. Here the battle of Saltville was fought, Gen. Dibrell commanding most of the fighting forces, repulsing Gen. Burbrige, who commanded a largely superior force, pursuing him into Kentucky and inflicting heavy loss. He then passed immediately with his command back through

East Tennessee, North and South Carolina and into Georgia, where in about two months from the time of starting on the raid he was fighting Gen. Kilpatrick on his raids toward the Savannah river, and harrassing Gen. Sherman's forces on the 'march to the sea.' It was here that we were in the saddle thirty-one days with scarcely any rations but sweet potatoes, which fortunately abounded in both Georgia and South Carolina."

William Vance married Elizabeth Boyd and located at Industry, Ill., before the Civil War. When the conflict came on one of his sons, John B. Vance, was living with his uncle, Jefferson W. Boyd, in Rock Spring Valley, this county, and teaching school at Pleasant Grove church. He immediately suspended his school and volunteered as a private Confederate soldier in Capt. H. H. Dillard's company. Later he become Captain of the company and met an heroic death at the battle of Perryville.

Stephen W. Brown was Register of Putnam county when the Civil War came on. Responding to the call for volunteers, Mr. Brown handed over his keys to Charles R. Ford, telling him to look after the office until his return. Four years later when Mr. Brown came back he found the county government in the hands of Union men and he and his comrades disfranchised.

AFTER THE WAR—With the return of peace, prosperity again smiled upon the new county and its rather insignificant seat of government, overshadowed as it was by the older and larger towns of Sparta, Livingston, Gainesboro and Carthage. Generally speaking, the post-bellum history of the town and county falls naturally into two distinct periods—before and after the coming of the railroad.

A HISTORY OF PUTNAM COUNTY

An early incident, rather amusing and one that the old timers never tired talking about, was the near riot at an exhibition of a traveling wagon show here soon after the war. A bunch of rowdies, filled with liquor and the spirit of lawlessness, took possession of the show and, displaying their pistols, announced that they were going to shoot the elephant! The audience, fearing that the pachyderm might become unruly during the execution, scattered wildly! After some difficulty and delay order was restored and the show was allowed to proceed. A few years later another show was broken up in confusion by the falling of the seats, in which several persons were severely injured. The historical value of these incidents is, they show that even that early enough people could be assembled in Cookeville to fill a circus tent.

Many of our older citizens remember the stage coach service to Nashville, requiring about twenty-four hours continuous travel (depending upon the roads), with relays at Chestnut Mound and Lebanon. John Reyburn, the old one-legged ex-confederate soldier, was the accommodating and careful driver on this end of the line for many years. As he would come rattling down the hill on the west side of the branch, often in the stillness of the night, the lonesome notes of his bugle would announce the arrival of the mail

The first bank to be established in the county was the Bank of Cookeville, opened in 1890, in a vacant store room on the south side of the Square. Its capital at first was only $20,000. J. Arnold was president, and J. W. Wright, cashier. R. L. Farley, bookkeeper, came a year later.

The first incorporated mercantile establishment in the county was the "Stock-Store," in Cookeville. The company was composed of J. Arnold, H. P. Davis, Hamp Moore and

S. G. Slaughter. They built a large two story frame house on the south side of the Square and did a thriving business until burned out in the early eighties.

David W. Dow's steam flour mill was the pioneer establishment in that line. It was located near the Glade Spring, south of West Spring street.

The oldest brick storehouse in the county is a little one-story structure on the north side of the Square in Cookeville. It has withstood fire and storm and the ever changing plans of man to maintain its original squattiness.

THE COUNTY SEAT—It appears to be generally believed that Maj. Cooke donated the land upon which the town of Cookeville was established, but such is not the case. Doubtless he would have gladly done so had the commissioners seen fit to make the location a few miles farther west. However, the land in question was purchased from Charles Crook, who made the deed to the Chairman of the County Court, the same being recorded on page 219, Book A, in the office of the County Register. This is one of the few record books to escape the courthouse fire. The deed reads as follows:

Charles Crook
       to
R. D. Allison, Chairman County Court

I, Charles Crook, have this day bargained and sold and do hereby transfer and convey unto Robt. D. Allison, Chairman of Putnam County Court and his successors in office forever, for the use and benefit of said County of Putnam, in the State of Tennessee, for the consideration of one hundred dollars to me paid, a certain parcel of land in the said State of Tennessee, Putnam County and District No. 1, it being the present seat of Justice of the said County, and containing by estimation forty acres, and bounded as follows: Beginning on a black oak and black jack pointers

A HISTORY OF PUTNAM COUNTY

in a conditional line between said Charles Crook and George and James Ramsey, running south fifty-two poles to a stake and black oak pointers, thence west eighty-four poles to a stake in a glade; thence north twenty-eight poles to a stake in a glade, thence east twelve poles to three hickories stake and black oak pointers, thence north sixty-six and one-twelfth poles to a stake and black jack pointers, thence east seventy-two poles to a black jack pointers in said conditional line, thence south with said line thirty-two and one-twelfth poles to the beginning.

To have and to hold the same unto the said Robt. D. Allison and his successors in office forever, I do covenant with the said Robt. D. Allison that I am lawfully seized of said land, have a good right to convey it and that the same is unincumbered. I do further convenant and bind myself, my heirs and representatives, to warrant and forever defend the title to the same against the lawful claims of all persons whatsoever to the said R. D. Allison and his successors in office.

In testimony whereof I have hereunto set my hand and seal on this the 2nd day of July, 1855.

(Properly acknowledged and registered same date.)

COUNTY GOVERNMENT

THE COUNTY COURT—Donaldson Allison was Chairman of the first Quarterly Court, which assembled Jan. 7, 1856. The members were: William C. Bounds, John Terry, Lee R. Taylor, R. H. Dowell, Moses A. Jared, James W. Baker, I. E. Ferrell, T. J. Lee, John Lee, John Madewell, Albert G. Davis, Isaac Lawler, J. D. Hyder, Isaac Clark, W. C. Johnson, Samuel Miller, Matthew S. Smith, J. W. Carlton, E. D. Crowell, R. G. Duke, James W. McDaniel, William Webb, Thomas Cooper, E. S. Thompson, James McKinney.

The Legislature in 1857 created the office of County

A HISTORY OF PUTNAM COUNTY

Judge for Putnam county, and Governor Andrew Johnson commissioned William C. Bounds as the first Judge. The office was soon abolished and the County Chairman plan adopted. Among those serving in this capacity were R. D. Allison, S. G. Slaughter, Jacob Henry, Benjamin Hitchcock, J. Arnold, J. N. King, John Tucker, J. J. Peek. In 1891 the Legislature again created the office of County Judge for Putnam county. T. L. Denny, of the Cookeville bar, was appointed to serve until the regular election in 1892, when W. G. Davis was elected. In 1894 J. W. Puckett was elected for eight years. H. D. Whitson was elected in 1902, and Sam Edwards in 1910. Judge Whitson was again elected in 1918.

The members of the present County Court are as follows:

S. E. Anderson, Albert Ashburn, J. T. Askew, Jr., J. L. Bilbrey, R. A. Bockman, J. J. Boyd, R. B. Capshaw, P. S. Cole, J. K. Flatt, J. S. Ford, L. W. Goolsby, H. T. Gragg, J. F. Hampton, J. W. Hickey J. D Henry, J. S. Herron, J. H. Hodge, B. C. Huddleston, Hugh Hunter, T. A. Hutcheson, T. B. Jackson, F. H. Jared, J. T. Jernigan, T. S. Johnson, J. W. Judd, P. L. Judd, A. W. Maxwell, J. N. McLoud, B. F. McBroom, W. R. McBroom, R. B. Officer, J. C. Parrett, J. H. Robinson, J. S. Robinson, J. W. Scott, J. D. Smith, R. B. Stewart, C. M. Stone, J. J. Sullins, W. S. Swallows, W. L. Swallows, John Tucker, W. M. Watson, Grover C. Whittaker, Tim Williams.

COUNTY OFFICIALS

Putnam County has been served by the following officials:

SHERIFF—Pleasant Bohannon, Robinson Dyer, J. H. McCully, W. J. Perkins, Campbell Bohannon, John Carr,

H. J. Brown, Charles Bradford, G. M. Moore, C. F. McCaleb, G. W. Alcorn, R. L. Jared, A. L. Weeks, R. L. Rash, L. F. Miller, Morgan Stout, J. M. Lee.

TRUSTEE—Joseph Pierson, Silas W. Gentry, Simon Maxwell, W. N. Gentry, J. M. Whitson, H. M. Nichols, W. J. Lewis, W. J. Isbell, J. H. Verble, Wheeler Harp, J. T. Pointer, O. N. Draper, D. E. Slagle, Haskell Womack, Mrs. Mary Denny.

REGISTER—William Baker, Stephen W. Brown, James Parsons, R. B. McDaniel, R. L. Lindsey, Russell Moore, C. R. Ford, J. Arnold, M. N. Scarlett, J. W. Puckett, S. F. Carr, W. P. Thompson, Norman Massa, S. S. Stanton, Haskell Grogan.

COUNTY COURT CLERK—Joseph H. Ray, Russell Moore, Gideon Anderson, E. H. Stone, H. P. Davis, W. J. Isbell, A. Bryant, John L. Ensor, W. H. Carr, D. C. Gossage, W. O. Watson, Algood Moore.

CIRCUIT COURT CLERK—William H. Carr, Curtis Mills, R. L. Gentry, J. H. Curtis, J. A. Carlen, J. A. Phrasier, L. J Garner, R. E. L. Proffitt, P. Y. Jared, Tom Scarlett.

In 1880 Henry P. Davis, of Cookeville was elected to jointly represent Putnam and White Counties in the General Assembly—our last floterial representative. Since that date Putnam County has elected the following representatives:

    1884—A. H. Young   1900—John B. Dow
    1886—Dr. J. P. Martin   1902—J. N King
    1888—J. C. Bockman   1904—J. N. King
    1890—H. B. C. Vaden   1906—Quimby Dyer
    1892—H. B. C. Vaden   1908—A. R. Massa
    1894—C. J. Davis   1910—A. R. Massa
    1896—Thomas Finley   1912—C. J. Davis
    1898—Thomas Finley   1914—E. L. Wirt

A HISTORY OF PUTNAM COUNTY

1916—T. W. Kittrell   1922—J. J. Sullins
1918—S. F. Carr   1924—T. A. Early
1920—J. N. King

These Putnam Countians have represented us in the State Senate: Holland Denton, R. S. Alcorn, A. W. Boyd, O. K. Holladay and George N. Welch.

Putnam County, as a part of the Fourth Congressional District, has been represented in Congress by Alvin Cullom, William Cullom, John H. Savage, W. B. Stokes, A. E. Garrett, H. Y. Riddle, S. M. Fite, E. I. Golliday, G. G. Dibrell, Benton McMillin, C. E. Snodgrass, M. C. Fitzpatrick, M. G. Butler, W. F. Clouse, Cordell Hull.

JUDGES—The following Chancellors have presided over our courts: W. W. Goodpasture, W. G. Crowley, W. W. Wade, B. M. Webb, T. J. Fisher, D. L. Lansden, A. H. Roberts, W. R. Officer. Our Circuit Judges have been Andrew B. McClain, N. W. McConnell, John A. Fite, W. M. Hammock, W. T. Smith, Cordell Hull, C. E. Snodgrass. The following have been elected Attorney General: H. C. Snodgrass, G. B. Murray, T. J. Fisher, Alfred Algood, M. G. Butler, W. R. Officer, J. R. Mitchell. Our Criminal Court was established in 1907 and J. M. Gardenshire was appointed Judge. He was elected in 1910 and again in 1918. In the spring of 1925 several changes took place in our courts. Judge Gardenhire resigned and Governor Peay appointed Albert Williams as his successor. The Governor also elevated Judge Snodgrass to the court of Civil Appeals, and made Attorney General Mitchell Circuit Judge. E. H. Boyd was appointed to succeed Mr. Mitchell in the office of Attorney General.

THE EARLY DAYS—Seventy-five or more years ago, before the days of Cookeville and Putnam County, a few widely scattered families had settled in the vicinity of the future town site. Dr. Benjamin Gabbert, the only practicing physician for miles around, lived just south of the present residence of T. D. Ford. Billie Ramsey lived near the Ramsey bluff, now in the eastern suburbs of Cookeville, while to the south were the homes of Michael Moore and John Barnes. Salem was the nearest church and near it lived several of the Huddlestons. To the north and west the land was so poor and barren that it was necessary to go several miles in order to find a house. Abraham Buck was one of the early settlers northwest of Cookeville. In those days White Plains was the post-office and nearest store. A branch of the State Bank was established at Sparta in the early years of the last century and for a long time this was the only banking institution in the mountain section of Middle Tennessee. Merchants for more than fifty miles around would bring or send their money to Sparta for deposit. Hundreds of thousands of dollars were carried in saddle-bags over the lonely roads leading through this territory, especially those to Gainesboro and Livingston. It is a distinct tribute to the high character of our pioneer citizens that but few robberies occurred in those early days.

The amusements of that time were generally house-raisings, log-rollings and corn-shuckings for the men, and quiltings for the women—an admirable combination of work and pleasure. At such gatherings, no lines of social cast were drawn and the younger set usually found a suitable place to stage an old-fashioned "break-down" of the Virginia Reel type. Of course a certain amount of liquid refreshment was served, but, strange as it may sound to us today, it was usually the older men, if any, who imbibed too freely. The music was furnished by one or more of the numerous good fiddlers found in almost every community. The uncorrupted Anglo-Saxon never turns to horns or drums or tinkling cymbals for his music, but is charmed by any stringed instrument—the fiddle above all. Among the old time pieces we might mention, "Arkansas Traveler," "Turkey in the Straw," "Natchez," "Apple Blossom," "Eighth of January," "Fishers' Hornpipe," "Ricket's Hornpipe," "Soldier's Joy," "Cheatham," and many others.

Two institutions, diverse in purpose but one in drawing power, flourished in ante-bellum days, to cease almost coincidently soon after the war. We allude to the camp-meeting and the horse-race, both mentioned elsewhere.

Another old time gathering that was usually well punctuated with fist-fights was the "Muster." For many years preceding the Civil War, all citizens of military age were required to assemble at convenient points to be instructed in the matter of drill, etc. The absence of the ladies with their restraining influence gave license to much loud swearing and general roughness. Onlookers would not permit the use of deadly weapons in these pugilistic encounters which were the never-failing source of much merriment.

Singing schools and writing schools both frequently broke the monotony of winter days, affording excuse as well as opportunity for the young people to get together. Experienced teachers went from one settlement to another and usually found good patronage. There were no public schools in those days and the subscription school rarely included more than a half dozen families, and very often was taught at some commodious and centrally located residence. Neighborhoods so fortunate as to possess a church building, however small and inconvenient, used this for schools.

Then, as now, the big game played on the school ground

was ball. The ball itself was commonly made of yarn thread of various degrees of density and weight. Various rules prevailed, but the usual arrangement provided for two batters, placed about thirty feet apart, armed with paddles about three inches broad. Behind each stood a combination catcher and pitcher. At every strike the batters must hastily change places. The rest of the school, scattered at various strategic points, were intent upon getting the ball and throwing it between one of the batters and the position for which he was headed. To thus "cross out" a batter meant to get his position. Also to catch a fly ball meant a position at the bat. "Town Ball," a later improvement, had one pitcher, a batter and catcher, and four bases. The players divided up into sides decided by the "wet or dry" method. It paved the way for baseball.

"Shinny" was a rather rough game for the big boys. Clubs were used to knock a ball from one shallow hole to another, opposing players resisting the progress of the ball. In the excitement of the game shins were often barked, hence the name. It must have inspired the creator of golf.

"Whoop and Hide" was another game especially popular with girls. "Blindfold" and "Tag" belong in the same class.

"Bull Pen" was strictly a boy's game, and a rather rough one, especially with a wet ball or one with a rock concealed in it. "Crack the Whip" was a bit rough.

Pitching horse shoes was another popular sport for the larger school boys, while "marbles" never ceased to interest young and old alike. All of which indicates that our grandparents were not so different after all.

Another characteristic of the early days before the Civil War was an excessive politeness between men. We have seen old letters which had passed between them that were effusive in the extreme and full of endearing terms. All

A HISTORY OF PUTNAM COUNTY

are familiar with the almost idolatrous homage paid to womanhood, by these chivalric old timers, but their formal softness toward each other, expressed in stereotyped phrases, provokes a smile now and then. For example, a Justice of the Peace at White Plains, back in the forties, made this entry upon his docket: "Blank, fined five dollars for a potation bout." There is something really Shakespearean in this polite description of a drunken fight! To say a thing like that calls for the Cavalier cast of mind and at the same time exhibits a fund of unspoiled English, such as only a Tennessee mountaineer, in his isolation from alien influence, could have preserved. "Potation bout," indeed! How many modern Justices could have thought or cared to phrase it so neatly?

Hyram Brown, an old and well-known citizen of Dry Valley, gave this information: "Cubit Whittaker built the first mill at the Brown's mill site in the early years of the last century. The government gave him a grant for thirty acres of land to encourage the enterprise. Billie Hunter was regarded by old citizens as the first settler in the Valley. He was the father of Dudley Hunter. The old home place later became the property of James Bartlett and is now owned by Alfred Bartlett. Braxton Hunter, originally from North Carolina, came from Kentucky to the Dry Valley in 1831. He was distantly related to Dudley Hunter, whose daughter, Sallie, he later married. Braxton Hunter was a highly educated man and spoke four languages. Two of his classmates in school were Henry Ward Beecher and Daniel Webster. He opened the first general store in the Valley in 1836. Mr. Hunter told me that when he came to Dry Valley in 1831 that Corder Stone was preaching at Brown's Mill Church, which he was reputed to have organized many years

A HISTORY OF PUTNAM COUNTY

before, probably as early as 1810. The preaching day was every third Sunday, which has continued down to the present without interruption. Back in the forties the church was moved across Falling Water to its present site, the ground being donated by my grandfather, Hyram Brown."

Mrs. T. W. Garrett, of Dallas, Texas, writes: "My grandfather, McClellen Jones came from Virginia and taught school at Nashville, in the year 1822 or 1823. When his school was out, he started back to Virginia and went as far as he could on the stage, then started walking and, somewhere near Cookeville, stopped to stay all night with a Mr. Rowland. He met Mr. Rowland's daughter, Elizabeth, and they were married within three weeks. Mr. Rowland gave them 100 acres of land near Cookeville for a home. Jones did not know one tree from another and Rowland had to show him what trees to build their log house with. In 1830 Mrs. Jones died, leaving five children—Elizabeth, William, John, Mary and Sallie. Later, Mr. Jones married Miss Newman. In 1854 or 1855 they sold their home and went to Kentucky.

Adam Massa came from North Carolina about 1828 and located on Falling Water near the falls. His son William, born in 1831, lived in that section until his death in 1891. Three sons of the latter—Dillard, Norman and Oakley—are business men of Cookeville.

Allen Young entered land on Indian Creek about 1820. His sons were John M., Lewis, Churchwell and Dock.

Prettyman Jones was one of the earliest settlers in Buffalo Valley. His sons were Buck, Prettyman, Wade, Robert and John.

A HISTORY OF PUTNAM COUNTY

CHAPTER FOUR

TOWNS AND VILLAGES

COOKEVILLE

Cookeville, the seat of government of Putnam County and its largest town, is situated near the geographical center of the county. It will be seventy-one years old in July, this year.

On February 11, 1854, ten commissioners were appointed by the Legislature to lay off the county site for the newly erected county of Putnam.

Maj. Richard F. Cooke was a conspicuous leader in the movement for a new county and it was largely through his efforts that favorable action was secured in the Legislature. There was no opposition to the proposition to name the county seat in his honor.

The first act of the Board was to authorize the Chairman of the County Court to purchase from Charles Crook a tract of forty acres of land, which was then laid off in town lots, excepting two and one-half acres reserved for the Public Square. The streets opened were Jefferson, East, Spring, Monroe, Glade, Narrow and Broad. The first lots were sold at auction July 13th and 14th, 1854, bringing from $25 to $167.25, the first one sold being at the maximum figure.

The first house built was a log grocery store, near the spot where the Cumberland Presbyterian church now stands. Very soon a temporary court-house was erected upon the lot now occupied by the residence of Mrs. A. W. Boyd. In the fall of 1854, Joe Copeland began the erection of the first courthouse in the middle of the Square, completing it in

January 1856. This was a neat but rather small brick structure. It was destroyed by fire a few years later, when, during the Civil War, a company of negro soldiers, enroute from East Tennessee to Carthage, camped in the courthouse yard. Early the next morning the courthouse was found to be on fire, whether of intentional or accidental origin was never clearly explained. After the war, David L. Dow, a capable builder, put up the old square brick house which stood until 1899, when it was burned with almost a total loss of all records and papers. The present courthouse, a very much larger and more costly structure, was completed in 1900, at a cost of about $25,000.

The old log jail, built in 1857, was destroyed by fire about forty years ago, and was soon replaced by the present brick building, which has since been considerably enlarged and improved.

The first stores in town were those of Douglass, Moore & Co., Terry & Son, J. W. Crutcher and J. C. Freeze. There were no women in town for more than a year and four young business men mentioned above, all unmarried, kept "bachelor's hall" in a log cabin on the lot where Mrs. Z. T. Hind's residence now is. In 1856 Mr. J. M. McKinney opened the first hotel in Cookeville, his wife and daughters being the first ladies to reside here. His grand-daughter, Josephine Crutcher, (Mrs. Charles Burton), was the first child born in the new town.

In 1856 Mrs. Cummins taught school in the house which formerly had been used as a temporary courthouse. Dr. Gabbert was the only physician, but Dr. Allison came a little later.

The first church was erected in 1857, and was used by all denominations, but years after was taken over by the Methodists. It stood just south of the present Richelieu

Hotel. It was a frame structure, about 25x40 feet in size, and served its day in many varied capacities—temporary courthouse, school house, political and other gatherings, as well as meeting-house for various kinds of preaching. It was sold in 1895, when the Methodists moved into their present brick church on Spring street. The Christian Church, erected in 1883, and the Cumberland Presbyterian, erected in 1881, burned in 1891 and rebuilt, were the next in order. Both congregations out lived their early quarters and are housed today in commodious modern structures. The Presbyterian, U. S. A., Church, a handsome brick structure on Dixie avenue, built in 1909, was the next addition to our churches. The last, the Baptist, one of the handsomest and best arranged in the town, was completed in 1923 The Nazarene congregation erected a temporary tabernacle on Oak street in 1923, where they worship.

Washington Academy, provided for by an Act of the Legislature, was started before the Civil War but was not completed until after the end of hostilities. It was a two-story brick and stood in solitary grandeur, the only house on the west side of the branch, excepting three or four widely scattered residences, the Hamp Moore place being the nearest, and farther west were the homes of Benjamin Hitchcock and Isaac Brown, while Hal Buck, the colored resident, lived somewhere in this wilderness of scrubby oaks and chinqueapin bushes. H. C. Fleming was the first teacher at the Academy. This old landmark was torn down in 1898, to make room for a much larger and more modern building, in which the Cookeville High School was opened in August, 1901. This building in its turn was demolished in 1921, and in its place stands the recently completed $100,000 public school building.

In 1881 the old Shaw hotel and other valuable property

on the south side of the square were destroyed by fire. Two years later the Reagan hotel and several stores were burned.

With the coming of the Nashville and Knoxville Railroad in 1890, the town took on new life. Wooden sidewalks and crossings were put down over the muddiest places and a serious attempt was made to "work" the streets. Up to this time the population was less than 400, but soon things began to happen in Cookeville. Civic pride was born and all worked in harmony. Cookeville grew rapidly from village to town dimensions. The location of the depot made possible the West-Side, and so substantial was this development that when the United States government in 1914 came to locate the site for our new $110,000 post office and Federal Court building it was placed west of the branch.

We cannot recount all of the accomplishments of the past two or three decades, but three things, in addition to those already mentioned, deserve notice. They are Dixie College (which paved the way for the Tennessee Polytechnic Institute), discussed in another chapter, and the Light and Water plants, both huge undertakings, involving a total outlay of about a quarter of a million dollars. The electric plant is located at Burgess Falls, eleven miles from town, and was built under the management of Mayor A. P. Barnes, while the Water plant is at the big spring on the farm of Mr. S. B. Anderson, 5 miles southeast of town, and has just been completed under the management of the present Mayor, Col. W. A. Hensley. These public utilities are owned by the town and are adequate for a population of 10,000, or more. The present population is very near 3,500. The assessed valuation of property in 1924 was $1,999,256.

Howard Hospital, on East Broad street, was completed and opened for the reception of patients in 1923, being the first general hospital in the county. Dr. W. A. Howard is the surgeon-in-charge. The people of Cookeville and Putnam County are very properly proud of this institution, which would do credit to a much more populous community.

These have been commissioned postmaster of Cookeville, in the order named: Curtis Mills, J. W. Crutcher, J. C. Freeze, James Goss, Braxton Hunter, W. H. Matlock, William J. Isbell, Joshua H. Brown, Henry P. Davis, Z. T. Hinds, John G. Duke, James M. Hinds, John W. Braswell, James M. Hinds, John E. Oliver, John G. Duke, Lewis J. Garner, Charles H. Whitney, Shelah D. Davis, John B. Dow, Norman Massa.

Several spasmodic efforts were made to establish a newspaper in Cookeville, beginning with the Monticello Times (later the Cookeville Times), published by Jonathan Buck. Jack McDowell, Dr. Baker, and others, made unsuccessful attempts in this direction. The "Chronicle" and "Echo" are long forgotten names of two early sheets. James Cope, of White County, conducted a small paper here for a year or so, back in the late seventies. Still later a Mr. Womack engaged in the newspaper game for a short time. The first really substantial newspaper was the "Cookeville Press," established about 1886, under the editorial guidance of Capt. Walton Smith. The N. & K. railroad was being projected about this time and the editorial columns of the "Press" strongly emphasized our natural resources. Rutledge Smith and Joe E. Gore conducted the paper under a joint partnership. About 1892 a stock company was organized for the publication of a new newspaper, "The Cookeville Courier." A year later the controlling interest in the corporation passed into the hands of John S. Denton and W. S. McClain, who had charge of the paper for about two years, when it was absorbed by the "Press." After the death of his senior partner, Mr. Smith continued the publication of the paper until other duties forced him to give up newspaper work. The "Press" ceased publication about 1910. "The Cookeville Citizen" was established in 1895 by W. S. McClain, who sold the paper to Charles Sims, of Sparta, about two years later. It too went to the newspaper graveyard in its third year. "The Southern Republican," owned by a stock company with money to burn, in a newspaper sense, was next to appear on the scene. With elaborate equipment and an imported editor, Mr. Carr, it made a strong fight, but it was soon over. Then John E. Oliver took charge and changed the name to "The Mountaineer"— but it would not go very long. Prof. Amonette Draper then tried his hand for a few months but the financial difficulties multiplied, and finally the plant was sold to Quimby Dyer, who changed the name to "News-Reporter." After about two years Mr. Dyer sold the plant to parties at Newport, Tenn. Walter A. Wirt opened a job printing office in Cookeville December, 1899, which he later sold to his brother Elmer L. Wirt. The business prospered and in 1903 Mr. Wirt decided to add a newspaper, "The Putnam County Herald," which has grown steadily along with the town and county. Its plant was totally destroyed by fire in 1908, without insurance, but it soon had a larger and better equipment. Today it is owned by E. L. Wirt and son, Ralph Wirt, and appears twice a week. "The Upper Cumberland News," the last to venture upon the tempestuous waters of local journalism, appeared in 1923. J. F. Gentry is the present editor. The "Herald" and the "News" are the only newspapers in the county.

The following is a summary of industrial and business enterprises of the town: Two flouring mills, two handle factories, two saw and planing mills, a hardwood floor

A HISTORY OF PUTNAM COUNTY

factory, an egg case factory, an overall manufacturing company, an ice factory, a large machine shop, three woodworking shops and four blacksmith shops. There are two wholesale grocery houses, one wholesale hardware company, one wholesale produce dealer and three wholesale and retail produce dealers, one cold storage plant, two large bottling works, a creamery and ice cream factory, three coal yards, two pole and cross tie yards, one broom factory, one bakery, one steam laundry and one marble yard. There are four large dry goods stores, three small general stores, four drug stores, two 5 and 10 cent stores, twenty-one grocery stores, four meat dealers, nine restaurants, ten garages, two wholesale oil and gas companies, three furniture and hardware stores, two watch repair shops, one photographer, three barber shops, an undertaker, an electrical dealer, two plumbing companies, two telephone companies, Western Union office, Express office, a shoe store, three shoe repair shops, one harness and saddle shop, a second-hand furniture dealer, three wholesale and retail lumber dealers, two newspapers, three hotels and two banks.

MONTEREY

The town of Monterey was laid out in April, 1893, by the Cumberland Mountain Coal Co., consisting of Messrs. J. H. and W. B. Ray and John W. Welch, local citizens, and John H. Onstott, of Guthrie, Oklahoma, and J. Ed Jones, of Springfield, Mo. The company acquired a large tract of beautiful level land just east of Standing Stone, and many lots were sold immediately after they were placed on the market. Mr. W. B. Ray built the first residence in the new town. The first general store was operated by the Coal Company. T. E. Goff, of Livingston, was the next to engage in the mercantile business. Today there are fifteen general stores in town, two drug stores, two hardware stores, and several smaller establishments.

The Bank of Monterey was organized in 1902, and the Union Bank and Trust Company began business in 1922.

The small frame school building, erected in 1896, was replaced by the present commodious brick structure, completed in 1908, at a cost of about $15,000. The Monterey High School was established about 1915. The average attendance in all grades is about 600.

Monterey is justly proud of her churches. The Baptist and Nazarene churches, both handsome edifices, are built of native mountain sandstone. The Methodist Church, the oldest in town, is brick and would be a credit to a much larger town. The Christian Church is a well built and nicely finished frame house.

The Monterey Lake Company owns a large tract of virgin forest just east of town, on which is an artifical lake covering about seventy-five acres. About eighty stockholders own lots on the water front and many summer cottages will doubtless be erected in the next few years.

The Monterey Hosiery Mill was started in 1919, and moved into its large new building in 1924, representing an investment of about $40,000.

The Monterey Hardwood Flooring Company is another large enterprise, doing an annual business of around $200,000.

Since the incorporation of the town, the following gentlemen have been Mayor: J. Ed. Jones, Emmett Goff, George N. Welch, Glen Flemming, W. J. Pugh, R. M. Brower, D. M. Speck and the present incumbent, J. W. Welch.

Monterey has been served by the following Postmasters: Jack Whitaker, J. N. Clouse, Byrd P. Allison, J. C. Walker and J. N. Clouse, the present official.

In 1924 Monterey ranked first in the nation in the shipment of golf sticks in the rough. This is also a good shipping point for other timber products.

Monterey has an adequate electric light system, and in 1924 spent $40,000 in street improvement, financed by a bond issue.

Six public roads lead to Monterey. The old Walton Road passes very near through the exact center of the town. This is the trade center for the eastern end of the county and parts of Overton, Fentress and Cumberland.

The Imperial Hotel was erected in 1904 by Gen. Wilder, a distinguished Federal officer of the Civil War, who spent his last years in Monterey.

Dr. W. C. Officer's Sanitorium for the treatment of throat and lung affections is nearing completion. It will contain about fifteen rooms and is ideally situated in a pine grove, overlooking the Calf Killer Valley.

St. Raphaels, an institution maintained by the Episcopal Church, under the management of Rev. A. C. Killifer, is doing a valuable work here, especially along charitable lines. It has a hospital department with a trained nurse in charge and no worthy person, however poor, is turned away. Instruction in nursing the sick is also given at the bedside in the homes of the very poor and illiterate. The institution was founded in 1916.

The population of Monterey is about 1800.

BAXTER

Baxter is the third town in Putnam County in point of population, and is situated on the Tennessee Central Railway, eight miles west of Cookeville. Previous to 1902, the small settlement was known as Mine Lick, but at that date the name was changed in honor of Jere Baxter. At one time the postoffice was named Ai. The present population is about 700.

The tract of land upon which the town of Baxter is situated was known for many years to old residents as the Lowe lands, and was several hundred acres in extent. Long before any thought of a town was entertained, Mrs. Bettie Wade bought a hundred acres of this land upon which she and Tobe Wade each built log cabins. This was about 1870. After a few years they abandoned the property and went out West. Later they sold it to Giles Bradford for $80 and some court costs, the consideration being about $100.

After the advent of the railroad in 1890, Joe Gentry bought a lot upon which he built and operated a general store. A little later Bob Oscar Gentry did likewise. These were the first business houses in the town. Next Joe Jones purchased three or four acres from a Mr. Elder and established a saw mill and distillery. Soon after this Mr. Brusher located an axe-handle factory—the large establishment that James A. Isbell later purchased and conducted. The saw mill and lumber business of Hill & Route was another big industry about this date. Cham Vestal established a furniture factory here about twenty-five years ago, employing some fifty operatives, and the venture was highly successful, but after his sudden death the business declined and was finally closed out. Mr. John E. Oliver built a large frame hotel which he conducted for several years and has since leased to other parties.

About 34 years ago the first school house was built, a small frame structure, which the town soon outgrew, and this was soon followed by a much larger building. This in turn gave away in 1922 to a handsome modern brick building in which the grammar school is conducted nine months in the year. The enrollment is about 300.

Baxter Seminary, a school of higher education, operated by the M. E. Church, is the pride of the town. It is discussed at some length elsewhere in this volume. The high school grades are also taught at this institution.

There are three churches in Baxter—Methodist, Church of Christ, and Presbyterian. All have regular services and Sunday School. The first church in town was built about 27 years ago by the Presbyterians, but was later sold to the Baptists, and finally torn down. The M. E. Church was erected about 1901 and the Church of Christ in 1905. The last named congregation moved into a new brick church about three years ago.

The Business Men's Club is a live organization and constantly on the look out for new enterprises.

Baxter was incorporated in 1915, with J. E. Oliver the first mayor. The present government is V. E. Nunnally, Mayor; V. B. York, Recorder, and four aldermen: W. R. Bradford, Lawrence Grace, D. B. Boyd and Jas. L. Sadler.

The town is fortunately situated in a beautiful section of the county and is the trade center for a large territory, including parts of Jackson, Smith, DeKalb and the Western end of Putnam. It is reached by one good pike and six graded roads. Corn, cotton and tobacco are the leading crops. The soil is especially adapted to the raising of vegetables and this is being done for the market more and more each year. The dairy industry is receiving much attention, as is also scientific poultry raising. Several small nurseries are operated in the vicinity of Baxter, and, collectively, do an annual business of about $75,000, with bright prospects for developing into a very large industry in the near future.

A HISTORY OF PUTNAM COUNTY

Baxter has one bank, two wholesale produce houses, one wholesale grocery house, one hotel and several boarding houses, a telephone exchange with long distance service, a Western Union Telegraph office, and an express and freight office. There are six general stores, two retail grocery stores, one drug store, one millinery store and one flour exchange. Two wholesale pole and cross tie companies have yards in Baxter. The handle factory exports tool handles to all parts of Europe. A large saw and planing mill does a good business. The Standard Oil Co., has a station here. A cotton gin is one of the newest industries. Also there are two or three restaurants, a garage, and possibly a few other small enterprises. The town maintains an electric light system.

ALGOOD

About December, 1893, Mr. S. A. Epperson, of Nashville, father of John A. Epperson, opened a branch of the Nashville Spoke and Handle Co., on the site of the future town of Algood—its first manufacturing enterprise.

In June, 1894, Mr. C. H. Rickman, of Hartsville, foreseeing the great possibilities in store for the country adjacent to Algood (not yet on the map), arrived on the scene ahead of the first train, purchased a lot on which he immediately erected a small frame building, and, associated with another hustler, Mr. John A. Epperson, opened the first store in the new town under the firm name of Rickman & Epperson. At this time there were only two other buildings in town, and both unfinished. The N. & K. railroad track had been laid about half a mile beyond town, but passenger trains had not begun to run. The new store, starting with only about $1500 worth of goods, had a wonderful trade from the beginning. Mr. Epperson managed the mercantile interests with consummate skill and ability, while Mr. Rickman was successfully engaged with the various outside activities of the firm.

In 1897 Pennock Brothers, of Nashville, established a large spoke manufacturing plant in Algood, and about four years later Mr. Walter bought an interest in the business and the firm was incorporated as the Pennock-Walter Mfg. Co. About 1902 Rickman & Epperson bought a large block of this stock, and in 1912 sold a part of it to Mr. Tom Clark. In 1923, A. G. Maxwell and R. L. Farley, of Cookeville, purchased the Rickman-Epperson interests.

Several changes have occured in the original mercantile firm of Rickman & Epperson. First, Mr. Rickman retired from the firm and Messrs. Wheeler Harp and Bob and Henry Pointer purchased stock in the business. Later, Mr. Epperson retired, and the firm has since been Harp & Pointer Co.

Algood was named in honor of the family upon whose lands it was established. Joel Algood built a residence there in 1857 and for many years the spot where the town was laid off was known for miles around as the "Algood old fields." This was a portion of a large tract of land originally entered by Henry McKinney and inherited by his son, James.

The Algood Brick Company produces a large amount of superior brick.

Algood is the southern terminus of the T. K. & N. Railroad, which extends to Livingston, a distance of about 18 miles.

In 1921 the 19th Civil district, of which Algood is the center of population and influence, voted a $30,000 bond issue for a new public school building, erected in 1922.

Algood has a bank, a drug store, hotel, and the average number of small business enterprises. The population is about 650.

BUFFALO VALLEY

The village of Buffalo Valley is situated on the Caney Fork River, in the extreme western end of the county, and takes its name from the large and fertile valley at the mouth of which it nestles. Tradition tells us that long before settlement had been made here that a rank growth of cane covered many square miles and that herds of buffalo would come down from the mountains to graze through the winter, when other pasturage was dead or scarce. An old tradition current among early settlers is that a huge buffalo was killed in the valley near the old Alcorn place, and from this circumstance the valley gained it's name.

The first business conducted here was the general store of Capt. James T. Exum opened very soon after the war— probably about 1870. Later Robert Alcorn opened a store. About the same time Samuel Young had a store at his farm, some three miles up Rock Spring Valley. Charles Burton's store on the ridge toward Chestnut Mound, some six miles distant, was the next nearest store for many years, until Alex Burton opened a store about three miles out on the ridge.

The first school and church building, dating from long before the Civil War, was the regulation log structure of that day. It stood about one mile up the valley near the Henry Jones place. Walker Brown was one of the first teachers. Finally a small frame building was put up nearby and used for several years. About thirty-five years ago the coming of the railroad infused new life into the community and a large two-story frame school building was erected—a decided addition to the settlement.

Dr. Sypert, (father of the late Dr. Ned Sypert, of Baxter), was the earliest physician. Awhile after the Civil War, Dr. W. M. Farmer moved over from Laurel Hill, DeKalb County, and spent a long life in the practice of medicine throughout the western end of the county. Dr. Samuel Denton, the present local physician, has been in active practice here for forty-four years.

The N. & K. railroad was completed to Buffalo Valley in 1890. Up to that time small steamboats made regular trips on the Caney Fork, as far up as Pinhook, carrying out many hundreds of tons of hogs, grain, lumber, etc. Rafts of logs were also common on this little river. The first railroad bridge was made with a turning span to allow the passage of boats, but after this was swept away by high water a few years later, boat traffic had entirely ceased and the present solid steel bridge was erected.

The Bank of Buffalo Valley was opened in 1912. Today in Buffalo Valley there are three general stores, three grist mills, two blacksmith shops, one pole and timber yard, one produce dealer and several live stock dealers. This is the largest hog market in the county, shipping an average of seventy-five cars of hogs every month. The lumber shipments total about fifteen cars monthly, with another ten of produce, poultry and miscellaneous items. The population is 134 by actual count.

Buffalo Valley has this unique distinction—it has no real estate for sale. This may sound strange to people who are fed up on boom methods and auction lot sales, but it is the literal truth. For years there has been no land for sale in the village of Buffalo Valley.

BLOOMINGTON

Scott Brown, 73, life-long resident of the Bloomington

community, says that his grandfather, Daniel Brown, came from North Carolina about 1830 and located one mile from the present site of Bloomington. His son, Jesse, (father of Scott) was a small boy at the time and, with other members of the family, slept in a large hollow tree while a cabin was being built. The cooking was done over a log fire in the open. They were very much disturbed at night by the howling of wolves. Mr. Brown's grant covered 900 acres.

The land where Bloomington stands was owned mainly by Matthew Kuykendall and Ridley Draper. The first house was built there, Mr. Brown thinks, about 1850, and is the one occupied by Meridith Gentry for many years. No one seems to know the origin of the name "Bloomington," but such a postoffice has existed as far back as Mr. Brown and other old citizens can remember.

Garland Kuykendall taught school here several years before the Civil War, and later Luke Gillem sold goods in the little school house.

Ridley Draper improved the spring about 1865 and made it something of a summer resort. He built several small cabins for his guests.

In the late fifties a small log church was built by the Methodists. Rev. T. R. Dodson, Rev. Alex Byers, Rev. Stephens and others preached here. Before the church was built religious services were held in the blacksmith shop.

Before the Civil War, Walton Road Allison, Carter Whitfield and Nahan Beck built temporary residences here in order to send their children to school.

Bloomington is the only village in the county that is situated off the railroad. Some years ago it was a considerable summer resort, but gradually declined. With a modern hotel it might come back.

A HISTORY OF PUTNAM COUNTY

At present there are three stores in the village, two grist mills and a saw mill. There is a nice public school building and two churches, at which there is occasional preaching. The population is about 200.

The largest enterprise is the Junior Military Academy, which occupies the old hotel property. For details see our chapter on schools.

DOUBLE SPRINGS

Originally, most of the land around Double Springs (so named because of two large springs in close proximity), was owned by Maj. Richard Cooke, although small tracts were early purchased by others. This was a postoffice about the time of the Civil War, but it did not aspire to be even a small village before the coming of the railroad. Daniel Hawes, who clerked in the store at White Plains, and Joseph Ray sold goods here at an early date. Later G. W. Judd & Son were local merchants. Here also was one of the ante-bellum "muster grounds," mentioned elsewhere. Among the older citizens we might name J. M. Barnes, Wood McBroom, J. M. McClellan, T. M. Scarlett and W. J. Steakley.

One of the large industries operated here before the days of prohibition was J. C. Barnes' steam distillery. At one time two large distilleries were running here at full capacity, the second one being operated by William J. Lewis. The last saloon in the county to close its doors was the "Lone Star" in Double Springs.

The Gainesboro and Sparta road crosses the old Walton Road at this place making it a good trade center. A large part of the railroad shipments to and from Jackson County passes through this village. This is also a good market for poles, crossties and timber products generally. Consider-

A HISTORY OF PUTNAM COUNTY

able live stock is shipped from this point.

At present, Double Springs has three general stores, a hotel, livery stable, garage, grist mill and a blacksmith shop. A very neat little church was erected a few years ago. The population is about 200.

SILVER POINT

Silver Point, situated at the head of Buffalo Valley, four miles north of Caney Fork River, was settled by several old families, notably the Mitchells, Maggards, Wallaces, Burtons, Pucketts and others.

Five public roads lead into Silver Point, making it easily accessible to a large territory of good farming country. It is a good shipping point, especially for timber products and live stock.

There is a good elementary school in Silver Point, and also two churches—Methodist and Christian. The colored people have a Christian church here.

Silver Point is a second-class postoffice, with four rural routes. There are three general stores and a grist mill in the village and a saw mill near by. The population is about 100.

BOMA and BROTHERTON, small stations on the railroad, each have general stores and a few residents. Both promise to grow into village proportions and some day may figure prominently in the county history.

Note—Our list of pioneers is by no means complete but we hope to add many names before the publication of the next edition of this work. Those possessing information as to pioneers not mentioned in this edition should send us the necessary data, so that they may be included in a future compilation by civil districts.

A HISTORY OF PUTNAM COUNTY

CHAPTER FIVE

SOCIAL DEVELOPMENT

SCHOOLS

Prior to 1873 public education in Putnam County, as in most of the sparsely settled sections of the State, was poorly provided for. The Legislature, at the earnest suggestion of Gov. John C. Brown, levied additional taxes for the support of elementary schools and otherwise revised our educational system. Still conditions were far from satisfactory. Putnam County children were receiving about three months of public school, ungraded and poorly taught in most instances, and very irregularly attended.

In the summer of 1886, the first teachers' training school ever held in the county was conducted at the old Washington Academy in Cookeville. Prof. T. P. Brennan, an educator of note from Nashville, was engaged to organize and teach this newly formed body, and under his able and sympathetic guidance a profound and lasting impression was made not only upon the teachers but upon the public in general, so that for many years thereafer the annual teacher's "Institute" was the big event in Cookeville. These annual meetings served to stimulate the teachers to do their best, and at the same time forcefully revealed to our County officials the imperative need for longer terms of school and better pay for the teacher. It may be truthfully said that the strong popular interest in education in this County had its inception largely in the old institutes, which in recent years have been supplanted by the summer school at the Polytechnic.

Ernest H. Boyd was elected Superintendent of Public Instruction in 1903, and served for eight years, retiring in

1911 to enter the law department of Cumberland University. He prepared a graded course of study and had printed at his own expense a manual for free distribution to teachers and school officials. The grading of the rural schools was the outstanding accomplishment of his administration. He was successful in bringing to Cookeville several annual State Teachers' Institutes, attended by hundreds of teachers. He abolished the antiquated log school houses, replacing them with substantial frame structures. Under his leadership the County Court steadily increased the taxes for the support of schools, and he not only had the full confidence of the Court but of the teachers and school directors as well.

At the annual Teachers' Institute held at Cookeville, in 1908, a committee on resolutions composed of Benton M. Stanton, Mrs. J. M. Dowell, Miss Sarah Mitchell, Miss Pearl Jared, Miss Vinnie Gentry, Elmore Gentry, Isaac Medley, J. R. Cole, J. M. Phy, A. W. Maddux and F. N. Billingsley, submitted a report which was unanimously adopted, and from which we copy this paragraph: "We endorse the administration of our County Superintendent, E. H. Boyd, under whose guidance the school terms of this county have been doubled in length, the school funds doubled, the teachers' salaries raised fully one-third, and the public school interests greatly increased. We urge him to become a candidate for re-election, and request our County Court to re-elect him, pledging him the hearty support of the teachers of Putnam County."

Prof. Boyd was one of the moving spirits in the organization of the Middle Tennessee Educational Association and was its first Secretary. The first meeting, which was held in Nashville, was attended by more than one thousand teachers. Prof. Weber, of the Nashville City Schools, was elected President. This has continued to be one of the leading educational organizations of the State.

Retiring from the office of County Superintendent in 1911, to take up the study of law, after eight years of faithful and efficient service, Prof. Boyd was succeeded by Prof. J. M. Hatfield.

Under the able administration of Supt. Hatfield, during the decade 1911 to 1921, the necessity for the establishment of a county high school was widely discussed, and finally came up in the County Court at the January term, 1914, for action. A motion to levy a tax of ten cents on the one hundred dollars worth of property for high school purposes was carried by a vote of 24 to 15. The Court elected the following High School Board: J. M. Jackson, E. M. DuBois, Dr. J. T. Moore, H. D. Whitson, J. F. Gentry and O. K. Holladay, with Supt. Hatfield ex officio. The questions of location, buildings, etc., were left with the Board and after several sites had been considered and delegations from Algood, Monterey and Baxter had been heard, it was decided to locate the Central High School in Cookeville and accept the offer of the trustees of Dixie College to turn over its buildings, campus and equipment for this purpose. Prof. T. K. Sisk was elected principal of the new school, which opened in Sept. 1914. In April, 1917, an effort was made in the County Court to reduce the school levy, but it did not succeed. The Legislature of 1921 removed all danger of such a backward step by making it compulsory for each County in the State to maintain at least one first-class high school.

The law establishing the Tennessee Polytechnic Institute at Cookeville provided that a thorough high school course should be given by the new institution, which was to take over the property of Dixie College. On June 23, 1916, the

County High School Board adopted the following resolution: "Resolved that the High School Board of Putnam County, pay to the State Board of Education, or the President of the T. P. I., what is left of the high school fund, after maintaining two other high schools in the county, approximately three thousand dollars, and that the same be used by said institution for the maintenance of a first class high school, to which all Putnam County students will be admitted free." Later a contract was entered into between the Board and the State, by the terms of which the Polytechnic receives two thousand dollars a year from the high school fund for this free service.

Other important features of Prof. Hatfield's administration were the consolidation of small schools, the erection of larger and more attractive school buildings, and the establishment of several two-teacher schools. During his term of office teachers' salaries increased about fifty per cent and the average term of school increased about one month. School Field Days were held annually and many Corn and other clubs organized.

Beecher Gentry was elected to the office of Superintendent of Schools in August, 1920, and re-elected in 1922. Perhaps the most important accomplishment of his administration was the establishment of uniform salaries for teachers, based upon experience, training and grade of certificate. Under the old order of things an inexperienced young teacher might receive even more money for his services than was paid to one older and better equipped.

The school term has been lengthened from five to seven months, and the budget has been made out and adopted for an eight months public school next year. This has been made possible, of course, by the great increase in revenue during the past four years, amounting to about $25,000.

New buildings, modern in every respect, have been

erected at Algood, Baxter, Wilhite, Thomas, and Salem. Additions and improvements have been made at Glade Creek, White Hall, Pleasant Ridge, Burgess, Mt. Pleasant, Double Springs, Bussell, Boiling Springs, Davis, Vaden, Mill Creek, etc.

1,500 to 2,000 new desks have been placed in the school houses of the county and this policy will be continued until all are supplied with the full number needed.

During Supt. Gentry's administration the daily attendance in the elementary schools has increased five hundred each year.

Baxter, Monterey and Algood have been raised to four-year standard high schools.

The total white scholastic population of the County last year was 3,987 boys and 3,689 girls, while the enrollment was 3,323 boys and 3,210 girls. There are 68 elementary schools and four high schools in the county for white children. The colored scholastic population was 118 boys and 173 girls, with an enrollment of 90 boys and 99 girls, in four elementary schools.

We give below the names of the various Superintendents of Public Instruction for Putnam County, with date of election of each:

1869—B. D. Hunter	1887—S. D. Upton
1873—B. M. Webb	1889—W. H. Carr
1876—H. S. Boyd	1893—A. N. Ford
1877—A. T. Anderson	1897—H. D. Whitson
1879—L. B. Matheny	1901—A. J. Chisholm
1883—A. Bryant	1903—Ernest H. Boyd
1885—T. L. Denny	1911—J. M. Hatfield

1921—Beecher Gentry

DIXIE COLLEGE

Back in 1909, ten determined and resourceful men put their heads and hearts together to work out some plan by which they might bring to Cookeville and the mountain country a much needed school of higher education. These men were Jere Whitson, Garrett A. Maxwell, A. G. Maxwell, R. L. Farley, J. N. Cox, J. B. Dow, Gid H. Lowe, T. D. Ford, W. B. Boyd and Jesse Elrod. Mr. Whitson was the recognized leader in this little group. Elder T. B. Larrimore, the well-known and beloved evangelist was present in many of the early conferences and was offered the presidency of the school, but saw fit to decline the honor, believing that some other man might lead it more successfully. To prove their faith, these ten men subscribed one thousand dollars each to start the movement.

About the time that these plans were being worked out and matured, the Legislature passed the law creating three normal schools, and Cookeville made a strong bid for one of these institutions, led by the Committee of Ten, which for the time suspended its efforts for a private school. However, the Normals went elsewhere and the Committee lost no time getting back on the job.

Prof. W. B. Boyd, a well-known and successful teacher of Celina, was made President of Dixie University—the first rather ambitious name of the new school. Dr. W. K. Azbill, of Cleveland, Ohio, was induced to come to Cookeville and spend several months assisting in planning and promoting the school. He was able and resourceful and rendered valuable service. Unfortunately, just about this time financial depression became acute, the Bank of Cookeville failed, and the school enterprise seemed on the brink of collapse. Nevertheless, Mr. Whitson held on and would not give up. On March 11, 1911, he and Mrs. Whitson deeded to the school a beautiful tract of land in the northern suburbs of Cookeville and actual construction on the main building was started at once. In the spring of 1912, President Boyd opened his school in temporary quarters in West Cookeville. The next fall session opened in the unfinished building on the school's campus, somewhat inconvenient and uncomfortable it is true—but the school was at home and its spirit was high. For some two years "Dixie" had a separate existence, then came the merger with the Central High School, which in turn gave way to the Tennessee Polytechnic Institute. Dixie College was in no sense a failure, and but for its short and aggressive career it is very doubtful if Cookeville could have secured the State institution.

TENNESSEE POLYTECHNIC INSTITUTE

The bill creating the Tennessee Polytechnic Institute passed the House on March 25, 1915, and two days later was signed by Governor Rye, becoming a law. Putnam County's Representative, Hon. E. L. Wirt, had charge of the bill, ably backed by a determined group of our leading citizens. Hon. John J. Gore, of Jackson County, led the fight for the bill in the Senate. The bill provided that Putnam County should donate fifty thousand dollars to the school and that Cookeville should give the sum of twenty-five thousand dollars. Enabling acts were passed a few days later, authorizing the county and town to issue the necessary bonds with which to meet their contributions to the school. These bonds were then voted, sold and the money paid into the State treasury in the record time. The trustees of Dixie College were to turn over their campus, buildings and equipment to the State, which they proceeded to do. During the legislative recess a bitter fight

A HISTORY OF PUTNAM COUNTY

was launched against the new school and when the Legislature reassembled an effort was made to repeal the bill creating it, and for awhile the situation was truly alarming.

The State Board of Education at an early meeting took up the difficult task of organizing the school. Prof. Thomas A. Early, of the Mississippi Agricultural College, was elected President, and during the four years of his incumbency the T. P. I. was established upon a firm and lasting basis.

The Legislature of 1919 appropriated several hundred thousand dollars for the erection of needed dormitories at the State Normals, including $100,000 for the Polytechnic. After some delay, the bonds were sold and the proceeds used in the erection of a large building for girls and extensive additions to the main building. These greatly needed improvements were completed and in use in 1923.

The present President, Prof. Q. M. Smith, was elected by the State Board July 1, 1920, to fill the vacancy occasioned by the resignation of President Early. He was re-elected in 1922,, and again in 1924. Under his able administration the institution has had a steady growth. The enrollment is slightly over 300. There are 19 full time teachers in the faculty.

In addition to the main building, the institution now has three large and well furnished buildings for boarding students, a fully-equipped machine shop, wood-working and other shops, poultry and agricultural equipment—a plant altogether representing an outlay of around $300,000.

At present, the last three years of high school instruction are given, but one will be dropped automatically each year, so that by 1928 only college work will be done at this institution. The State appropriation for the T. P. I. is about $50,000 a year.

BAXTER SEMINARY

In the spring of 1909, Prof. H. C. Coleman, Principal of the Baxter Public School, began agitating the need of a High School department, and at his earnest solicitation Prof. C. W. Coleman, a graduate of Dayton University, was induced to come to Baxter and join him in the organization of the "Baxter Institute." Fifty students were enrolled for the first term. The financial backing, however, was hardly sufficient, and at this juncture Rev. J. D. Harris, presiding elder of the Baxter District of the Methodist Episcopal Church, conceived the idea of bringing to his home town an institution of higher education, under the management of the Educational Board of his church. His plan, which at first seemed highly visionary, was explained to a large mass meeting of Baxter citizens, and in 1910 was officially confirmed by the Central Tennessee Conference and the Board of Education. "Baxter Seminary" was chartered under the laws of Tennessee, and in addition to the higher branches gives a standard high school course. A majority of the Trustees are laymen. But for the determined and aggressive leadership of Rev. Harris the movement could hardly have succeeded. Nevertheless, the splendid pioneer services of the Colemans should not be underestimated or ignored. They, too, deserve great credit.

Diplomas are given in Religious Education, Home Economics, Smith-Hughes Agriculture, Teachers' Training, Music, Commercial Courses and Physical Training.

The campus, about twelve acres in extent, is beautifully situated in the southern suburbs of Baxter, a part of it in virgin woodland. The main building, a large concrete structure, is well arranged and adequate for present needs. The Boy's Dormitory, a well planned brick building, has just recently been completed, and a like structure for girls is contemplated. Gifts of money and equipment have come from friends in various States. Young people with limited means are given every possible opportunity to work their way through school. The faculty is composed of 6 teachers and the average enrollment is about 100.

The well-known educators who have held the position of President are Samuel F. Ryan, F. S. Ditto and P. R. Broyles. The present incumbent, Harry L. Upperman, a gentleman of scholarly attainments and an untiring worker, has made several successful drives for needed funds and under his management the school is growing and prospering.

JUNIOR MILITARY ACADEMY

In 1920, Col. L. L. Rice, one of the foremost educators of the State, realizing the disadvantage of associating younger boys with boys of high school age, established a Junior school at Bloomington Springs, this county, to affiliate with his school for older boys located at Lebanon. At first the new school was known as the Castle Heights Junior School. Later Col. Rice disposed of Castle Heights but retained the Bloomington school, the name of which was changed to Junior Military Academy. In 1922 a permanent business arrangement was entered into with Major Roy DeBerry and under his management as Headmaster the school has had a rapid growth. The enrollment is the fall of 1922 was only ten cadets, but seventeen were enrolled in 1923 and forty in 1924. A capacity enrollment is expected by 1926. The school is nationally advertised and maintains a very high standard, giving entire satisfaction to a list of patrons representing nineteen states. It is the only school of its type in the South that devotes its entire attention and resources to boys doing work in the grades below the high school.

A HISTORY OF PUTNAM COUNTY

PROF. SAMUEL B. YEARGAN

No history of the educational development of Putnam County would be complete without some extended mention of the career of Prof. Samuel B. Yeargan, who came to us from Murfreesboro in 1883, and spent the best years of his life teaching in our leading schools, public and private. He was married to Miss Clementina Reagan on December 20, 1886, to which union four children were born—Reagan L. Yeargan, of Harriman, Mrs. C. B. Byrne, of Bisbee, Arizona, and Misses Elizabeth and Louise Yeargan, of Cookeville, all of whom survive him. He died at his home in Cookeville, on October 23, 1920, in his seventieth year, mourned by thousands who had come under the spell of his magic influence.

Prof. Yeargan was particularly successful with ambitious young people who really desired an education. Upon such his inspiring lectures, coupled with his clean life and intense passion for truth, made a profound and lasting impression. For years he taught a private select school in Cookeville, whch became widely known, and at which hundreds of young men and young ladies received a liberal education. No man who has ever lived in our midst was more helpful and inspiring. Truly, he was a great man and a great teacher.

CHURCHES

THE BAPTISTS—In 1804, fourteen churches of the Green River (Ky.) Association withdrew to form the Stockton Valley Association, with eight churches in Kentucky and six in Tennessee. This Association is still in existence and covers Fentress, Pickett and Morgan Counties in this State. In 1813, some of the southern churches withdrew and formed the Caney Fork Association. It is thought by some that the old Caney Fork (Brown's Mill) church may have been one of these churches. There are no authentic records to prove this, however, as nearly all of these early documents have been lost.

Later, the Caney Fork Association divided over doctrinal questions, the branch retaining the original name (Caney Fork) becoming Two-Seeders or "Hardshells" in doctrine, while from the other party two Associations were formed, namely, Freedom Association, still in existence and affiliating with the state organization of Baptists in Kentucky, and Stone Association, composed of the old Caney Fork church and the Cane Creek Baptist Church, both in Putnam County. This last Association took the name of two of its leading preachers, Charles Stone and his son, Thomas Stone, who have many descendants and kinsmen now living in Putnam County. Organized in 1866, Stone Association remained independent until 1918, when it asked admission into the regular Tennessee Baptist Convention and was received. Since then the Cookeville Baptist Church, which was a part of the New Salem Association of Smith County, and originally established in 1873 (but for several years almost extinct), was reorganized on the first Sunday in February, 1913 with nine members, and is now in the Stone Association. The Monterey Baptist Church, which was a part of the Riverside Association, transferred to the Stone Association in 1924.

There are three small churches in the west end of the county which are still in the New Salem Association, and one in the southern section of the county in the Union Association. All told, there are eight regular Baptist Churches in Putnam County, with a membership of about 2,000. In addition, there are two very small Baptist churches calling themselves United Baptists, and there are a few small churches, five or six in Putnam County, that withdrew in 1920 to form another association, called Stone Association of Free-Will Christian Baptists. Dodson Branch Church, just over the line in Jackson County, is in the Stone Association as well as Poplar Springs across the line in Overton, and also one or two in White and Cumberland counties. The members of the Stone Association in Putnam County are as follows: Cookeville, Monterey, Caney Fork, Cane Creek, Free Union, Poplar Grove, Macedonia, Rocky Point, Sand Springs, Verble, Wood Clift, West Union, Algood, Allen's Chapel. The three churches in the New Salem Association are Boma, Hopewell, Nash's Chapel. Boiling Springs is in the Union Association.

CUMBERLAND PRESBYTERIAN—On August 20, 1867, following a noted revival conducted in the Washington Academy building, by Rev. Jesse E. Hickman and Rev. Stephen Davis, the Cookeville congregation of the Cumberland Presbyterian Church was duly organized. Dr. J. M. Goodpasture and Jesse Pendergrass were elected Ruling Elders, and the former was also made clerk of the session, which position he held until his death.

In November, 1891, this congregation lost its church building by fire, but soon thereafter the present commodious structure was erected. The original building was a large and handsome one-room auditorium, built in accordance with the then prevailing type of church architecture, and occupied the present lot, fronting the east.

Rev. J. R. Goodpasture served as pastor at three periods, aggregating twenty-five years. He was sincerely loved by all and left a profound impression for good upon the community.

The present Ruling Elders of this congregation are J. P. Hamilton, Ezra Davis, Morgan Davis, S. B. Caruthers, A. C.

A HISTORY OF PUTNAM COUNTY

Hooper, H. C. Lansden, Will C. Davis and B. M. Hudgens. The present pastor is Rev. B. W. Covington.

The pastors previous to the division in 1909 were: Reverends Jesse E. Hickman, James K. Lansden, William P. Smith, James T. Williams, J. R. Goodpasture, T. A. Wiggington, W. J. King, C. H. Rayburn, W. V. McAdoo, P. M. Collins, J. R. George, C. W. Estes, J. W. Sneed, A. F. Zeigel, M. Seals and John T. Price.

The Ruling Elders for the same period—1867 to 1909—were Dr. J. M. Goodpasture, Jesse Pendergrass, S. K. Phillips, John T. Pendergrass, Henry P. Davis, J. C. Freeze, C. N. Wheeler, Dr. J. F. Dyer, Jesse Arnold, Holland Denton, E. D. Staley, J. H. Barbee, Walton Smith, A. W. Boyd, Thomas Finley, Prof. N. J. Finney, Judge D. L. Lansden, S. S. Webb, S. A. D. Smith, H. D. Whitson and J. H. McCawley.

THE PRESBYTERIAN, U. S. A.—In 1909 there was a division in the Cumberland Presbyterian congregation of Cookeville over the question of organic union with the Presbyterians, U. S. A., and those who favored this course withdrew and purchased a beautiful site on Dixie avenue (the old Mills home) on which they proceeded to erect a beautiful and modern church building.

The first pastor of the newly organized church was Rev. J. T. Price, then came Rev. B. V. Riddle, who was succeeded by Dr. A. J. Coile, who in turn was followed by Rev. L. T. Lawrence. The present pastor is Rev. B. T. Watson.

The Ruling Elders are J. M. McCormick, C. E. Wilson, C. P. McClanahan, A. D. Pendergrass, Dr. J. F. Dyer, L. D. Bockman, R. R. Bockman, R. H. Harding, E. H. Boyd, S. S. Webb, Quimby Dyer and J. C. Darwin.

The Deacons are J. G. Duke, W. H. Johnston, Bedford

A HISTORY OF PUTNAM COUNTY

Webb, Eugene Jared, J. B. Thompson, J. B. Goodpasture and Grover C. Boyd.

Other officials are E. H. Boyd, Church Clerk; Prof. M. H. Barnes, Supt. of Sunday School; O. E. Cameron, Church Treasurer; J. B. Goodpasture, Sunday School Secretary; and Eugene Jared, Financial Secretary.

METHODIST—Because of their distinctive organization, so well adapted to sparsely settled communities, the Methodists easily led the other churches in pioneer times. Pleasant Grove in the lower end of the county, Salem in the middle division, and Standing Stone on the mountain were early strongholds of this faith, with many smaller churches coming later. However, the steady influx of population from the Carolinas, where the Baptists were especially strong, soon made this denomination an aggressive, but not unfriendly, rival. Soon the Cumberland Presbyterian and Disciples of Christ began to gain adherents and establish congregations. These four denominations practically included all of the religiously inclined.

The Camp meeting was largely a Methodist institution and many noted camp-grounds were annually thronged by great crowds eager to drink in the impassioned words of long-winded exhorters.

The Methodists have strong congregations at Cookeville, Monterey, Algood, Baxter, Pleasant Grove and other points —eleven in all at present. The membership totals about 1,800. The Cookeville District was created in 1921, and the Presiding Elder resides at the district parsonage in Cookeville.

The northern branch of this church has its largest congregation at Baxter and a small one at Summerfield, a short distance north of Cookeville. The Presiding Elder of the Baxter-Tullahoma District resides at Baxter.

A HISTORY OF PUTNAM COUNTY

The pastors of the Cookeville church have been: Randolph, Parks, Freeman, Cherry, Harmer, Blanton, Clenny, Sanders, Sabastian, Allison, Moores, Patterson, Freeman, Jared, Alexander, Ford, Herriges, Jarvis, Stellar, Smotherman, Baker, Gilbert, Nackles, Baird, Hudgens, Allen, Doss, McClaren, Tinnon, Craig, Walker, Cook and Wood.

PLEASANT GROVE CHURCH.—One of the oldest Methodist congregations in the Upper Cumberland section is that of the Pleasant Grove Church, in the 11th civil district of this county. Before the Civil War, Pleasant Grove was one of the noted camp-grounds in this part of the State and the annual camp-meetings were attended by thousands of people. The location is a beautiful and picturesque beech grove in the head of Rock Spring Valley. Religious services were regularly conducted here for about a century.

Several years ago the congregation decided to move the church building from its original and historic site to a near-by point on the ridge, on the Nashville road. A few years later, this splendid frame building was replaced by a modern brick structure—the most valuable and commodious rural church building in the county.

School was taught regularly at the old Pleasant Grove church from pioneer times until many years after the Civil War. It was truly a community center for old and young. Many large families grew up in the old Pleasant Grove church. These names are conspicuous in its annals: Jared, Byrne, Hughes, Holladay, Young, Boyd, Carlen, Huddleston, Nichols, Maddux, McKinley, Leftwich, Denny, Taylor, Stanton and Evans.

The Pleasant Grove congregation has given to the Methodist church a number of prominent ministers, among them Jasper, John H., and B. B. Nichols, three brothers, all of whom are now dead. John H. Nichols was the author of numerous religious books which have had a wide circulation. He was a very able and remarkable man.

Rev. G. D. Byrne, a brother-in-law of the Nichols brothers, after fifty years of labor in the ministry, is now a superannuated member of the Tennessee Conference and resides at Monterey.

Among the other preachers of marked ability sent out from this congregation were the following: The Jared brothers, Wade and James, the former dead and the latter a prominent member of the Missouri Conference; the three Ensor brothers—Dow A., and S. M.—members of the Tennessee Conference,—and John O. Ensor, of the Missouri Conference; N. B. Taylor of the Texas Conference; and Frank P. Jernigan, Missouri Conference.

The oldest rural Sunday School in the county is that at Pleasant Grove, and it has always been one of the best. James A. Boyd, now living at an advanced age, was Superintendent for twenty-five years. Altogether, there is no more historic church in the county or in this section of the State.

DISCIPLES—This Church is especially strong in the middle division of the county. Smyrna, established in 1830, is perhaps the first congregation in the County. Elder E. G. Sewell, who was for many years a leader among those of his belief, was a native of Putnam County and a member of the Smyrna congregation. He was one of the founders and an able editor of the Gospel Advocate, of Nashville, Other distinguished ministers have gone from this pioneer congregation.

The Cookeville congregation was organized about 1880. The first church building, a small frame structure on Washington avenue, is still standing and has been used for several years as a wood-working shop. The present home of this church is a large brick edifice on Broad street. The congregation numbers about 400. The present pastor is Elder J. Pettey Ezell.

There are congregations at Algood, Monterey, Baxter, Double Springs, Bloomington, Antioch and perhaps at other points.

NAZARENE—The largest congregation of this belief is at Monterey. Rev. A. P. Welch, the pastor since its organization, has labored faithfully for many years and has lived to see his efforts bear much fruit. The splendid stone church in which this congregation worships, costing approximately $40,000, is a monument to their zeal and enterprise.

The church at Cookeville, organized some five or six years ago, is the second largest and is growing steadily.

There are congregations in other sections of the county.

FRATERNAL ORDERS

I. O. O. F.—Mt. View Lodge, No. 179, Independent Order of Odd Fellows, was instituted December 19, 1873, the Charter members being Dr. J. P. Martin, J. J. Finney, J. H. Brown, J. J. Mills, Dr. J. F. Dyer and H. J. Brown; C. C. Comee, D. D. G. M., of Livingston, officiated. There were four initiations at the first regular meeting—Dr. J. B. S. Martin, Dr. L. R. McClain, George Judd and E. D. Staley. For many years the meeting place was the Masonic Hall, the second floor of the old Washington Academy. Since its organization, several hundred members have been added to the local lodge of this great Order, and at one time the membership reached the two hundred mark, but owing to the establishment of other lodges in the county and the consequent withdrawals and transfers, the average paid-up membership for several years has been about 175. 52

members have died and have been buried with the honors of the Order. Thousands of dollars have been paid out for sick and burial benefits. Mt. View Lodge owns its own hall, a splendid two-story structure on East Broad street, costing about $5,000. The present veteran Secretary, Dr. L. R. McClain, has served his lodge in this capacity for more than forty years. Cookeville Encampment, No. 45, a higher branch of the Order, was instituted in 1874. Sylvan Rebekah Lodge, No. 58, the ladies' branch, was instituted in 1896.

There are lodges of this order at Monterey and Baxter. The lodge at Algood was consolidated with the parent lodge at Cookeville a few years ago.

MASONS—A Masonic lodge was organized in Cookeville soon after the town was established, but the old records appear to have been lost or destroyed. (Could some one help us out here?)

Cookeville Lodge, 266, F. & A. M., was organized December 6, 1866. Among the earlier members were Joel Algood, W. P. Chapin, H. Denton, H. H. Dillard, John Chilcutt, J. C. Freeze, D. L. Dow and Anderson Sloan.

The Masonic Hall is the building purchased by the local lodge from W. D. Sloan, in 1920, situated on the South side of the Square. The membership is about 200. The Commandery and Chapter, branches of this fraternity, have thriving lodges here. About 40 Putnam County members belong to the Shrine.

There are three other Masonic lodges in the county—Monterey, Baxter and Rock Spring.

Also, there are about 25 Scottish Rite members in the county.

Cookeville Chapter, 152, Order of Eastern Star, was organized January 27, 1914.

A HISTORY OF PUTNAM COUNTY

WOODMEN—Cookeville Camp, 12248, Modern Woodmen of America, was organized July 5, 1906, with seventeen charter members as follows: H. W. Apple, M. H. Borden, L. M. Bullington, S. R. Brinkley, L. H. Byrne, W. H. Chapin, M. T. Davis, E. B. Duke, A. W. Elrod, G. N. Guthrie, C. N. Elrod, B. H. Phillips, W. S. Rash, Griffin Smith, W. C. Wade and E. B. Wilcox. The membership has grown to 150, and the total insurance carried is $236,000. This Camp has never lost a member by death. The Clerks since the organization have been: E. B. Duke, 1906-7; R. H. Wirt, 1908-17; M. M. McDonald, 1918; Charles S. Stanton, 1919-19—. A member of this camp, Dr. G. N. Guthrie, was the first delegate from Tennessee to the National head camp, and was also a state delegate to the two succeeding head camp meetings.

SONS OF TEMPERANCE

Division No. 21, Sons of Temperance, was organized at White Plains, November 20, 1848. The officers were: Daniel W. Hawes, W. P; James M. McKinney, W. A.; Lee R. Taylor, R. S; J. L. Goodbar, A. R. S; Jonathan Buck, F. S. T; J. T. H. Huddleston, C; D. P. Hughes, A. C; J. C. Freeze, I. S; T. T. Pointer, O. S; Rev. T. C. Quarles, Chaplain.

From an old minute book of the Rock Spring Division, No. 239, Sons of Temperance, we gather that this Division met regularly from 1849 to 1856. E. F. Douglas appears prominently in the record, as does Charles R. Ford, Recording Secretary. The following names appear on the roll of members: N. S. Apple, John H. Young, John M. Null, William Whitehead, Thos. J. Kilman, Charles A. Huddleston, Joel Fitzpatrick, W. J. Huddleston, Jesse S. Carr, Allen Young, John H. Carr, C. B. Reynolds, Samuel Cameron,

Enoch Fisher, Phillip Sadler, John H. Amonette, Martin Whitten, James Plunket, J. W. Allen, George Carter, E. F. Douglass, L. H. Betty, James E. Hogan, A. H. Farmer, L. P. Reynolds, William Lester, J. F. Colvert, Thomas J. Gill, Joseph Johnson, John E. Farmer, James Carlen, William B. Holladay, Charles R. Ford, Brice B. Jared, Isaac H .Huddleston, Samuel A. Moss, M. W. Sypert, A. M. Betty, S. Petty, J. Rowland, Franklin Palmer, H. W. Carlen, George Carter, G. F. Marchbanks, R. B. Benson, George W. Whitten, P. Sadler.

It may be news to some of today that not all of the old timers were given to much strong drink. No doubt the minutes of the White Plains Division, if available, would show an equally imposing array of good citizens. Perhaps, also, there were other Divisions in the County, of which the writer has not heard.

THE COUNTY ASYLUM—Martin Laycock was superintendent of the County Poor House, situated two miles north of Cookeville, in the years before the Cvil War, so we are told by Mrs. Mary Quarles, 84, widow of John Quincy Quarles, a life long resident of that vicinity. After the war, Mr. Quarles was superintendent for awhile, followed by Ned Chote, Denton Quarles, Cant Chism and perhaps others for short periods. Then came the administration of Christopher Columbus Davis for a period of about ten years. All of this time the institution was a constant expense but the inmates were few. The buildings were small and cheaply constructed and the farm prouded very little of anything. In 1890, the County Court voted to purchase from Samuel Sliger a larger and more productive farm, about five miles north-west of Cookeville, and make an effort to place the institution upon a self-supporting basis. This

A HISTORY OF PUTNAM COUNTY

was under the administration of County Judge Denny. The average number of inmates for the past twenty years has been about ten, mostly very old and infirm people. Very few children have been cared for at the Poor House, and only one negro, so far as we have been able to learn. The following superintendents have served since 1890: William A. Rippetoe, William King, Andrew Robinson, W. W. Brown and A. H. Hawkins, the present incumbent. Benton M. Carr of Cookeville, is the Poor House Commissioner, elected by the County Court. About $2,500 have been spent for improvements during the last few years, including running water, etc. The farm produces enough to reduce the up-keep of the inmates to about $180 a year for each.

The Fisk Road, running north and south through Putnam County, was surveyed by Moses Fisk. It ran from Sparta to Hilham, and was later extended to Burkesville, Ky. It was first called the Meridian Road.

The Dyers and Pippins located mainly in the Blackburn's Fork country about 1820. The names of the Pippin pioneers were Red, Willis, William, Kinch and Henry. The Dyers were James, William, Johnnie and Samuel. The last named entered land in the Mine Lick region, while Johnnie settled on the Walton Road, opening up the farm known later as the Whittaker place.

B. L. Scarlett writes from Anita, Iowa: "I am the last member of Capt. Dillard's Company left. H. H. Horty is the only survivor who was at the surrender at Bentonville, N. C. In the Company, nine died of disease, twenty-four were killed and thirty-one were wounded."

A HISTORY OF PUTNAM COUNTY

CHAPTER SIX

INDUSTRIAL DEVELOPMENT

THE N. & K. RAILROAD—The outstanding industrial event in the history of our county was the construction of the Nashville & Knoxville Railroad. The road was financed and built by Mr. A. L. Crawford, millionaire iron manufacturer, of New Castle, Pa., with whom was associated his four sons, Andrew and James, of Terre Haute, Ind.; Hugh, of St. Louis; John, of New Castle, and a son-in-law, Ellis S. Hoyt, also of New Castle. These men were all manufacturers and leaders in the industrial world.

It appears that Mr. Crawford, realizing the ultimate development of the vast coal fields of the Cumberland Plateau, had invested largely in undeveloped coal lands lying in Putnam and Fentress counties mainly. This was back in the early eighties and at this time he had no thought of building a railroad. Later, however, he conceived the idea of bringing this coal to market. In this decision he became the greatest benefactor of the upper Cumberland country—Putnam County, in particluar. We hope some day to see a fitting monument to the memory of A. L. Crawford, erected in the courthouse yard in Cookeville. The appreciation of our people is general and genuine, and all that is needed to express this sentiment in enduring stone is the leadership of some civic organization.

After deciding to build the road, Mr. Crawford perfected such traffic arrangements as he could with the N. C. & St. L. Railroad and established physical connection with that road at Lebanon. Surveying corps were in the field early in 1887. Dirt was first broken in actual construction at Watertown in October, 1887, and grading contractors rushed

A HISTORY OF PUTNAM COUNTY

construction in both directions from this point. Early in 1888, Lebanon was reached and track-laying was ready to begin. Mr. David Dorman, of Alliance, O., a valued and greatly esteemed employee of the Crawfords, was selected to bring the first engine to the new road, which he did in March, 1888. In June, Edward E. Dorman, of Allegheny, Pa., a son of David Dorman, brought the second engine to the road. The third engine was put into service in February, 1889, with William Fiddler, of Gallatin, in charge, and the fourth was added in August, 1890, with Dock Dean of Louisville at the throttle. A little later Joe Barbee, who had helped survey the road, and was its oldest employee in point of service, was assigned to an engine.

The track was completed to Cookeville, July 4, 1890. On July 17th, a well patronized excursion train was run from Cookeville to Lebanon, connecting with a train to Nashville. This train returned to Cookeville on the 19th and began a regular daily schedule. The excursion was on account of the State Democratic Convention which nominated John P. Buchanan for Governor.

The first conductors on the road were Will and Homer Roberts, brothers, of New Castle, Pa., and later came George Lumsden, Ed Brown, Will Duke and Rufus Gollithan.

The Civil Engineers in charge of construction from the inception of the road to its completion were, successively, Maj. Negley, Charles Allison, Capt Fitch and R. J. Moscrip. A. Vandivort was the first Superintendent, followed by T. W. Stewart, shortly after the completion of the road to Cookeville.

The old passenger depot at Cookeville was a two story frame building about 20 by 40 feet, with waiting room and baggage room below and offices above. It stood just a few feet south of the track, at what is now the crossing of Broad and Cedar streets. The freight depot was on the north side of the track, a little west, and in the street just about in front of the Citizen's Bank. These structures were torn down by the T. C. Railroad and replaced by the present brick depot and large freight house.

The Dormans, father and son, retired after several years of continuous service on the road. Both had purchased and improved property in Cookeville and established their homes here. David Dorman died April 23, 1898, and his remains were laid to rest in the Cookeville cemetery. About this time E. E. Dorman, recognizing the need of a first-class machine shop in this rapidly developing territory, established an enterprise of this character which has grown to considerable proportions. Mr. Dorman tells us that when the road was being built, before stock gaps could be put in, that it was a common occurrence for the train to stop at a fence across the track while the crew removed the bars, which they immediately replaced after the train passed. This was a part of the daily program, and happened not once, but many times.

Mr. A. L. Crawford, the master mind of the enterprise, died at his home in Pennsylvania in 1890, just about the time his railroad reached Buffalo Valley. Many of our citizens feared that his untimely death might seriously interfere with the completion of the road, but such was not the case. His sons and other associates, realizing how much he had set his heart upon this pet undertaking, resolved to carry out his plans without modification. However, after the completion of the road to Cookeville, construction was suspended for about three years.

After the extension of the road up the mountain in 1893, to the new town of Monterey, there was another interval in building. The next extension was to the Crawford coal

A HISTORY OF PUTNAM COUNTY

fields in Overton County.

TENNESSEE CENTRAL RAILWAY—In 1893, Jere Baxter capitalist and promoter, of Nashville, backed by a group of St. Louis business men, organized the Tennessee Central Railroad which then purchased the Nashville & Knoxville Railroad from the Crawfords and proceeded to build an extension of the line from Monterey to a junction with the Southern Railway at Emory Gap, and later at Harriman. The new company made every possible effort to purchase the Lebanon branch of the N. C. & St. L. Railway, but, failing in this, was forced to build its own line from Lebanon into Nashville. The Tennessee Central was burdened with debt from the beginning and unable to place and keep its track in first-class condition and provide adequate equipment. Besides, it was "bottled up" and at the mercy of connecting roads, so that it was only a question of time until it was forced into the hands of receivers. The step was taken in 1912, necessitated by the tangled finances of the road, and lasted until its reorganization in 1922, when it was purchased by a syndicate and the name changed to Tennessee Central Railway Company. Freed from the incubus of debt the road then entered upon an extensive program of improvement. New and heavier steel was laid upon the entire system, and the road bed greatly improved, also many powerful new engines were added along with hundreds of new freight cars. All through passenger trains carry new steel coaches and Pullmans. The road is prospering and making every effort to serve its territory.

The N. & K. Railroad was chartered March 21, 1884. The Tennessee Central Railroad charter was dated August 25, 1893, and under it Col. Jere Baxter built the line from Monterey to Emory Gap. The Tennessee Central Railway was organized June 14, 1897, and the line was built from

A HISTORY OF PUTNAM COUNTY

Lebanon to Nashville. The Nashville and Clarksville branch was organized April 16, 1901. The Tennessee Central Railroad Company, organized May 1, 1902, embraced these various roads. The name of the road since its reorganization, February 1, 1922, following the termination of the receivership, has been the Tennessee Central Railway Company.

GAINESBORO TELEPHONE COMPANY—This corporation, the largest independent company of the kind in the South, was organized at Gainesboro, Tennessee, in 1896, by Messrs. Geo. W. Stephens, J. T. Anderson, Jas. N. Cox, G. A. Maxwell and Gid H. Lowe. The headquarters were moved to Sparta in 1897, and the chief offices were there for eleven years. In 1908 the company purchased valuable property on Broad street, in Cookeville, and established its permanent home office here. The present officials are: A. G. Maxwell, President; Jas. N. Cox, Vice-President and General Manager; G. A. Maxwell, Vice-President; R. L. Farley, Vice-President; S. Hayden Young, Secretary and Treasurer; Charles Stanton, Auditor. This company owns and operates about one thousand miles of toll lines in Tennessee and Kentucky, covering thirty counties, with twenty-six exchanges and more than one hundred employees. The Capital Stock is $400,000, and the annual volume of business is around $200,000. The company is constantly extending its territory and has just recently purchased the Central Telephone Company operating in Scott, Fentress and Morgan counties.

THE HOME TELEPHONE COMPANY—The Putnam County Home Telephone Company was organized April 18, 1910, with the following officers and directors: V. E. Bockman, President; Dr. S. D. Davis, Secretary; J. T. Shirley, W. C. Maxwell, W. F. Tilley, W. L. Huddleston, R. A. Elrod, W.

R. Porter, J. S. Lewis. The Cookeville exchange serves about five hundred subscribers with a total of 570 telephones. Exchanges are also operated at Algood and Baxter. The present officers are A. P. Barnes, President; J. M. Dowell, Vice-President; B. C. Huddleston, Secretary; T. B. Jackson, General Manager; E. H. Buck, Treasurer. The authorized Capital Stock is $5,000.

FARMER'S MUTUAL FIRE INSURANCE CO.—This Putnam County institution was organized in May, 1914. The first policy was issued June 16, 1914. The incorporators were B. C. Huddleston, H. D. Whitson, M. L. Farris, B. P. Pointer and J. N. King. The first Board of Directors was as follows: H. D. Whitson, President; B. C. Huddleston, Vice-President; J. N. King, Secretary; E. H. Buck, Treasurer; S. M. H. Taylor, Joe C. King, E. H. Davis, M. E. Whitson, C. Bohannon, W. R. Nicholas, John West, M. L. Farris. The present officials are B. C. Huddleston, President; C. Bohannon, Vice-President; T. A. Hutcheson, Secretary; E. H. Buck, Treasurer; W. R. Nicholas, M. L. Farris, S. C. Huddleston, J. A. Green, T. B. Jackson, Benton Carr, M. L. Stewart. This company has about one million dollars of insurance in force. The average annual assessment for ten years has been around 30 cents per $100, and some years it has been as low as six cents. This is one of the best co-operative plans ever introduced into the county, and has saved our farmers a very large sum of money. It is perfectly safe, because every policy holder is backed up by every other one in the association. Insurance is written on farm property only and at the actual cost of operation.

PIKES—Putnam County was first among the mountain counties to realize the value of better roads. In 1909 the county voted by a large popular majority to issue $150,000 for good roads, and in 1911 another $100,000 was voted for the same purpose. The following gentlemen were elected by the County Court to serve as a Good Roads Commission: W. B. Ray and Lewis Johnson for the Eastern Division, J. N. Cox, C. H. Rickman and J. W. H. Terry of Middle Division and James A. Isbell, J. H. Jared and Henry Jones for the Western Division. The need for roads was so great and the popular clamor for them so insistent that soon more miles were projected than could be properly finished with the money appropriated. Of the 90 miles graded only about 30 were given a complete macadam surface. But the fatal error was the failure of the County Court to provide an adequate maintenance fund to keep the roads in repair. For several years after the construction of these pike roads, no repair work of any kind was done upon them, although it was clearly evident that they were rapidly deteriorating. Soon ruts were cut in the surface through which water finally reached the foundation, with disastrous results. This costly experiment was an economic crime—nothing less.

Our latest activity in the matter of good roads was the participation of the county in building the State-aid road from the Overton County line to Cookeville, by way of Algood. The road, now nearing completion, is a broad highway, asphalt surface, and will be maintained by the State. Its cost to Putnam County will total about $69,000. Other State-aid roads have been projected in the county, on which construction will probably begin this year. The Sparta road and the Cookeville-Nashville road are now being maintained by the State.

OIL—Just after the close of the Civil War, mainly in 1866-67, a number of producing oil wells were in operation on Spring Creek, near the Overton County line. The wells were not very deep, but the oil was of a high grade. It was

A HISTORY OF PUTNAM COUNTY

barreled and hauled in wagons to McMinnville for shipment by rail and some even hauled to Butler's Landing, on the Cumberland River. About this time the discovery of extensive oil fields in the north so depressed the price of crude oil that it was no longer possible for the operators in this and Overton counties to continue production under the then existing transportation handicap. The wells, machinery and all, were simply abandoned. No precautions were taken to prevent flooding by surface water, and after a time the oil was displaced and ceased to flow. Old citizens tell us that several of these wells were real gushers. On one occasion Spring Creek was covered with oil for miles, not only killing the fish but many geese and ducks as well. The oil was fired and burned for many days.

COUNTY FAIRS—The first Agricultural Fair in Putnam County was organized in 1856, two years after the erection of the county. It was located on the property now owned by C. E. Wilson, on Dixie avenue, in Cookeville. This was not a very large undertaking and, like most other enterprises of that day, was abandoned during the Civil War. From a copy of the constitution of the Society, printed in 1860, by William Baker, we take the following list of stockholders: R. D. Allison, W. Z. Buck, Ridley Draper, J. C. Freeze, C. Mills, J. W. McDaniel, Joseph Pearson, Isaac Buck, John Barnes, R. E. Fain, Wesley Harvey, W. R. Hutcheson, J. S. Allison, J. M. McKinney, T. T. Watson, John Bohanon, W. A. Terry, John F. McDaniel, James McKinley, Isaac E. Ferrell, H. G. Huddleston, V. M. Terry, C. R. Ford, B. F. Brinley, W. W. Cowen, C. F. Burton, W. F. Williams, S. D. Burton, J. A. Ray, W. C. Bounds, R. Dyer, R. F. Cooke, J. L. H. Huddleston, Russel Moore, W. B. Gordon, Pleasant Bohanon, J. W. Crutcher, John Terry, Curtis Terry, W. M. Marchbanks, J. C. Apple, O. P. Apple, Peter

E. Goodwin, L. P. Conaway, H. H. Dillard, Joseph Terry, W. P. Dowell, John Chilcutt, Joel Algood, S. H. Maddux, T. J. Maddux, B. F. Gardenhire, J. H. Moore, J. T. Terry, Elijah W. Terry, Sam F. Patterson, Rollen Terry, Jasper Terry, Jonathan Buck, Jr., J. R. Rollins, H. W. Sadler, W. Baker, Burton Marchbanks, A. E. McBride, A. H. Hoover.

The By-Laws contain this paragraph: "The price of admission, single tickets, will be sold at the office at 15 cents each, good for one admission only; boys under twelve years old 10 cents; small children and negroes free."

In 1871 a new Fair Association was organized, and for several years very creditable exhibitions were held. Six acres of land, purchased from J. G. Stewart and D. L. Dow, located just north of Tennessee Polytechnic Institute, cost the Association $10 per acre. The improvements cost less than $1,000. The first officers were: Holland Denton, President; H. H. Dillard and D. L. Dow, Vice-Presidents; Jonathan Buck, Secretary; A. Sloan, Treasurer; C. J. Davis, J. H. Moore, S. G. Slaughter, J. H. Windle and A. Laughbaugh and P. Bohannon were Directors. The old records of the first annual exhibition—October 18-19-20, 1871—show that the following captured premiums: J. H. Quarles, James Robinson, A. Harpole, Mrs. C. R. Ford, Mrs. Lucinda Denton, Mrs. M. Freeze, Mr. E. Pullen, J. H. McCulley, Miss Belle Marchbanks, Mrs. E. D. Staley, Mr. A. Sloan, Mrs. O. F. Terry, Ruark & Bradford, I. C. Burgett, Miss Kate Douglass, Miss L. Young, Mrs. L. D. Gray, Mrs. Trogden, Mrs. Blatchford, R. F. Pippin, Curtis Mills, J. C. Freeze, R. Draper, T. T. Pointer, Charles Burton, W. Y. Marchbanks, B. H. Moore, Nathan Cox, J. W. Terry, D. L. Dow, John Terry, J. G. Stewart, W. A. Terry, W. J. Mills, T. A. Scudder, H. S. Wells, W. P. Dowell,

A HISTORY OF PUTNAM COUNTY

J. E. Copeland, J. R. Hamilton, H. H. McCarver, M. Moore, Willie Sloan, Rollen Terry, Green Wilhite, W. S. Marchbanks, Jeremiah Whitson, Jr., Stephen D. Pointer, J. H. Stone, W. M. Marchbanks, Lawson Sims, W. H. Barnes, James T. Draper, C. E. Bohannon, B. F. Ferguson, David Grace, J. E. Matheny, J. D. Terry, M. W. Cummins, E. W. Terry, John Cornwell, P. Bohannon, J. C. Nichols, A. A. Reagan, R. W. Southard, John M. Ballard, C. J. Davis, G. R. Dowell, P. M. Tinsley, Arthur McDaniel, Eli Sims, Lee Gilliland, H. C. McCarver, Martha C. Dowell, Paulina Hunter, Jane Terry, Sue Armstrong, Lucy Moore, Parazetta Terry. The minutes of later exhibitions reveal the names of hundreds of well-known citizens, but our space is too limited for the entire list. After a few years financial difficulties began to multiply and soon the Association ceased to function. The grounds were sold at auction and bid in by Mr. Jere Whitson. As stated, they are now a part of the campus of the Tennessee Polytechnic Institute.

The Third Fair Association was launched in 1896. It, too, was a stock company and after some years the shares were bought up by a few individuals. The present owners are A. P. Barnes and Rutledge Smith. Annual exhibitions have been given regularly since its establishment. Large crowds attend from this and adjoining counties.

The fourth venture in the Fair realm was made by a group of farmers and stockmen in 1923. Later they were incorporated as the Putnam County Agricultural Fair. The annual exhibitions are given in and around the Courthouse, in Cookeville, and no admission is charged. The premiums are paid by business men and other public spirited citizens, supplemented by Putnam County's share of the State appropriation for the aid of county fairs.

COUNTRY STORES—Before the Civil War the largest

general store in the county was the establishement of Mr. Charles Burton, on the Walton Road, in the west end of the county, near the Smith County line. Mr. Burton was an active merchant here for more than fifty years, and was a man of wealth and influence. He owned the first carriage brought to the county.

In 1877, Mr. Jere Whitson opened a store at Jeremiah, near the Overton County line, and within a few years was selling more goods than any other store in the county, Cookeville included. Later, Mr. A. P. Barnes, a salesman, bought a half interest in the business, which continued to thrive. Mr. Whitson moved to Cookeville in 1890 and later sold his interest in the Jeremiah store to Wheeler Harp. After some years Mr. Barnes also sold out and became a citizen of Cookeville. Finally, the Jeremiah store was moved to the new town of Algood and reorganized as Harp & Pointer Brothers. Both Mr. Whitson and Mr. Barnes are present prominent business men of Cookeville.

BANKS—First National, Cookeville, organized 1910; capital $50,000; surplus, $45,510. D. C. Wilhite, President; O. E. Cameron, Cashier.

Citizens' Bank, Cookeville, organized 1914; capital $15,000; surplus, $26,500. S. B. Anderson, President; H. S. Hargis, Cashier.

Bank of Monterey, organized 1901; capital $30,000; surplus $25,000. W. B. Ray, President; J. S. Woodford, Cashier.

Union Bank and Trust Co., Monterey, organized 1922; capital $40,000; surplus $650. John W. Welch, President; Jas. P. Welch, Cashier.

Bank of Algood, organized 1910; capital $15,000; surplus $2,000. J. T. Pointer, President; C. E. Hampton, Cashier.

A HISTORY OF PUTNAM COUNTY

Baxter Bank and Trust Co., organized 1906; capital $15,000; surplus $5,000. Lawrence Grace, President; V. B. York, Cashier.

Bank of Buffalo Valley, organized 1912; capital $5,100; surplus $900. Samuel Denton, President; J. E. Evans, Cashier.

The combined deposits of these institutions is slightly above $1,600,000.

IRON AND POWDER—Killebrew's "Resources of Tennessee" (1874), page 883, contains this interesting statement: "Pilot Knob, two miles south-west of Cookeville, is reported to be very rich in iron ore. The beds of brown hematite extend all around its base, and probably underlie the entire mountain. But little effort has been made to develop it. In the vicinity of Cookeville we saw some good ore but were unable to estimate the quantity. In the neighborhood of Hudgen's Creek is another extensive bed of ore similar to the hematite found in this part of the State. Several years ago there was a bloomery on Falling Water four miles south of Cookeville, which, with the imperfect machinery used, yielded about forty per cent of pure iron. The ore was obtained in the neighborhood and from Pilot Knob. With good machinery it would doubtless yield from fifty to sixty per cent. When better facilities for transportation are provided, the manufacture of iron will doubtless assume great importance. We are informed that there is an excellent quarry of marble at Pilot Knob, but have seen no specimens. It has been used for tombstones to a limited extent."

Notwithstanding Mr. Killebrew's excellent reputation, we were at first disposed to doubt the bloomery story, until it was confirmed by several old citizens. We have seen evidences of excavations for ore on the farm of Mr. Oscar Ferguson, in the eastern suburbs of Cookeville, in a group of surface holes, the ore evidently being in small pockets. All that seems to be known about this enterprise is traditional and that it was some time before the Civil War probably in the forties.

But Mr. Killebrew tells us something else, even more surprising. In speaking of the falls along the course of Spring Creek, he says: "The falls at Waterloo, where there was once a large powder manufactory, being the most important." This also we have been able to verify, but the exact date is a matter of conjecture.

Mr. Potter Greenwood, an old and well-known citizen of the northern part of the county, tells us that he barely remembers the old powder works at Waterloo. He says that it was operated by a man named Nat. Dodd. One day while the powder was being dried an explosion occurred which wrecked the plant and badly burned John Roberts, one of the workmen, blowing him a considerable distance. Mr. Greenwood thinks this was about 1854, possibly a little earlier. He also tells us that salt was made there at the same time. Large kettles, filled with water containing considerable salt, were used to evaporate the excess water and leave a residue of salt.

CLIMATE—The Bureau of Soils of the Department of Agriculture, Washington, D. C., issued a survey of Putnam County, March 10, 1914, from which we take the following statement:

"The climate of Putnam County varies somewhat in the different sections, the high altitude of the Highland Rim and Cumberland Plateau having quite a perceptible influence upon the local conditions. The summers are pleasant, being nearly free from oppressive sultry periods. As a whole they are too short to allow the growing of cotton as a staple crop. The winters are short and usually mild, except for occasional cold snaps, during which the mercury seldom falls below zero. Light snows of short duration occur every winter.

"The mean annual precipitation is 49.8 inches and the normal annual temperature 59 degrees F. During the winter months the rains are heavier and of longer duration than in in summer, a considerable part of the precipitation during the growing season coming in the form of showers.

"The early, warm days of spring and the erratic occurrence of killing frosts cause the fruit crops to be uncertain, except where special care has been used in locating orchard sites. The average dates of the last killing frost in the spring and the first in the fall are April 4 and October 23, respectively."

THE WORLD WAR

Putnam County met every demand and went " over the top" at every call. The total registration of men under the selective draft was 4,074. Of these 1,018 were exempted on account of dependency, 377 were accepted at camp, 369 were accepted for general service, 151 were disqualified, 58 exempt on account of agriculture, 31 placed in limited service and 13 exempted for industrial purposes. Thirty-three men met death in the service of their country.

The War Department at Washington advised us recently that it had no list of veterans according to place of residence, consequently it could not supply us with a roster of Putnam County soldiers. The Adjutant General of Tennessee has a record of all Tennessee soldiers, but these have not yet been arranged by counties. He promises to do this as soon as the Legislature sees fit to increase his office force. The American Legion of Putnam County could have furnished a partial list, but one so incomplete that we deem it best to postpone the matter for a later and larger edition of this work. There is no danger that the names of these heroes will be lost to history and we can afford to wait for the correct roster.

The Local Board of Selective Draft in this county was composed of G. W. Alcorn, Rev. A. J. Coile and Judge Sam Edwards. Later, Mr. A. P. Barnes succeeded Mr. Alcorn, and Dr. Z. L. Shipley succeeded Judge Edwards.

Maj. Rutledge Smith, of Cookeville, served as Chairman of the State Council of Defense, with headquarters at Nashville, rendering valuable service.

Hickman Whittaker was one of the most famous of our early fiddlers, with Jack Slagle a close second.

Dr. Bluford Finley, in Stamp's Cove, was the only physician for many miles before the Civil War.

One of the prominent early physicians of Cookeville was Dr. J. M. Goodpasture, who moved to the new town in 1857.

There were toll gates on the much traveled Walton Road in its early days. Robt. Officer kept one just east of Standing Stone.

In the list of past Mayors of Monterey the names of T. B. Holloway and and R. W. King were inadvertently omitted.

About the middle of page 75 this line should have appeared: "Mr. T. G. Settle, of Nashville, was associated with Mr. Draper."

Elsewhere it is stated that the Cookeville jail burned about forty years ago. This is incorrect. The fire was in October, 1894, soon after Sheriff-elect McCaleb moved in.

An early citizen of the Double Springs community was Jesse Barnes, Sr., who located there before the Civil War. His children were Jesse, James, Mary Jane, Frances, Minerva and Celia.

A HISTORY OF PUTNAM COUNTY

CHAPTER SEVEN

GEOLOGICAL

The rich alluvial region contiguous to Buffalo Valley, washed largely from the ragged escarpment of the Highland Rim, which towers above it to the east, makes Putnam County's contribution to the Central Basin. The numerous conical hills with the narrow valleys and coves all point to long continued erosion. The towering cliffs of the Caney Fork are beautiful exposures of thick bedded limestone—dark blue crystalline and fossiliferous. Above this is a ragged formation of thin bedded, knotty limestone, immediately beneath which (and about two miles up the valley) a vein of flourite outcrops. We are not informed as to how extensively this deposit has been investigated. The next formation of interest is the Chattanooga black shale of the Devonian period, some forty feet thick in this section of the state. It contains about ten gallons of oil to the ton, is rich in pyrites and other compounds, and is the source of our sulphur waters.

Coming on up the hill toward Silver Point, we encounter first the Tullahoma and then the Ft. Payne chert (splendid road building material), and then comes the massive St. Louis limestone—the floor of the Highland Rim. The last belongs to the Mississippian division of the Carboniferous period.

What valuable mineral deposits might we reasonably expect to find in this particular locality? Certainly we need not look for coal or copper or other precious metals, but there are a few very valuable things that might be found here in paying quantities. The upper horizon of black phosphate rock is just above the Chattanooga black shale, and we have good reason to expect outcrops of this valuable rock along the face of the eastern section of the Highland Rim. Indeed, a rather promising deposit was found in a ravine about one mile south of Boma several years ago, and mining operations were carried on for a time, but ended in failure—for what reason we are unable to state. A careful survey might reveal a thicker deposit and one more easily mined.

At several points along the brow of the Rim small outcrops of manganese oxide have been found in the Ft. Payne chert. This, too, could exist here in paying quantities.

The Highland Rim, a comparatively flat rim of land surrounding the Central Basin, averages about 750 feet above sea level. It is the largest of the eight natural divisions of the State and makes up nearly half of the area of Putnam County. Its cap formation is the St. Louis limestone which supports an unusually deep clay soil, often 30 or more feet in thickness and containing fossils and water worn quartz pebbles from old river deposits. The towns of Boma, Baxter, Double Springs, Cookeville, Bloomington and Algood are situated upon this formation. Except along the small streams where the soil has been washed away, very few rocks are exposed, and they are usually found undisturbed.

The very best grade of brick can be made from the clays of this region and more enterprises of this character would do well. A cheap grade of pottery was manufactured in a crude manner and upon a small scale near Cookeville several years ago, and there are numerous deposits of such clay in this vicinity. There is a strong demand for just this character of pottery, and it would easily absorb any reasonable output. This particular clay is well adapted to the manufacture of flower pots and drainage tile.

A HISTORY OF PUTNAM COUNTY

About 18 years ago a small quantity of a very compact blue-white limestone of fine texture was taken from a quarry about three miles north of Algood. At first it appeared to fulfill all of the requirements of first class lithographic stone, but the presence of scattering fossils and calcite crystals rendered it of little value for this purpose although a few small pieces were used with excellent results. It is entirely possible that at a greater depth, or perhaps at another situation, a purer variety of this rare stone might be uncovered. To say the least of it, nothing better has yet been found in the United States, since practically all of our lithographic stone is imported from Europe—chiefly Germany.

Just east of Algood, where the ragged spurs from the face of the Brotherton bench of the Plateau reach down to the Rim, a very fine Oolitic limestone, nearly white and testing around 98 per cent lime carbonates, lies practically uncovered in enormous quantities. Unless there are certain impurities not showing upon the surface, this stone is just as fine in every way as is the great deposit at Crab Orchard, where a large lime manufacturing plant has flourished for many years. Not all limestone will make good lime by any means, but if that near Algood will meet the requirements it is a very valuable asset indeed.

During the Carboniferous Period the region that is now the Cumberland Plateau was a swampy land, covered with rank vegetation, and was alternately above and below water, as its various sedimentary rocks plainly tell us. The entire region was later upraised from around sea level to its present altitude of about 2,000 feet.

The Mountain limestone, resting directly upon the St. Louis formation of the Rim, averages about 500 feet in thickness and is the floor for the Bon Air coal measures—the lowest of the three coal horizons of the Plateau. Above this is the varied Pennington formation with its numerous thinly stratified shales, limestone and sandstones, and finally, the massive conglomerate sandstone which caps the Putnam county part of the Plateau. The Tracy City and Brushy Mountain coal measures are above us.

Near the western escarpment of the Plateau the coal deposits thin down and become pockety and unreliable. Drift mining was attempted at Monterey but soon abandoned. Still there is a vast amount of fine coal in Putnam County, but no extensive mining is carried on except at Ravenscroft, near the White county line. Recently, however, the Putnam Coal Co., opened a very promising vein in the 5th Civil district, about 12 miles from Cookeville. They propose to market their output with a fleet of trucks, we understand.

A few miles east of Monterey there is a vein of superior white clay about two feet in thickness, resting upon the Rockcastle sandstone, and with slight overburden. This clay was extensively used by the Harley Pottery Co., at one time. However, their plant at Nashville was destroyed by fire some seven or eight years ago and never rebuilt. No doubt a pottery enterprise at this point would prove successful if properly managed.

We would not overlook the beautiful and evenly bedded sandstone near Brotherton and Paragon, where many quarries might be opened and building stone produced upon an extensive scale.

The census of 1920 gives the population of Putnam County as 22,231, but there is every reason to believe that it exceeds twenty-five thousand today. The assessed valuation of all taxable property is 1924 was $8,712,120. The area is 404 square miles, divided into 2,983 farms. There are 49 miles of railway in the county.

A HISTORY OF PUTNAM COUNTY

CHAPTER EIGHT

BIOGRAPHICAL

By Quimby Dyer

In the foregoing chapters of this history many well known citizens have been mentioned, especially those who were active from pioneer times down to the Civil War period. The half century immediately following that bloody conflict produced many strong and interesting characters. Among these were the following:

DICK LATTA LANSDEN, son of Hugh Hill Lansden and Lee Ann McGee Lansden, was born at Baker's Cross Roads, on May 15, 1864. His parents resided in Cookeville for several years but later returned to White County. Young Lansden was admitted to the bar and for awhile practiced law at Sparta. Here he married Miss Helen Snodgrass, daughter of Hon. H. C. Snodgrass. He was elected Chancellor in this District in 1902, and was regarded by the bar generally as one of our ablest Judges. In 1910 he was elected to the Supreme Court of Tennessee and served with distinction as Chief Justice until failing health forced his retirement in 1923. He died at Montgomery, Ala., on August 8, 1924, and is buried in Cookeville.

GEORGE HAMPTON MORGAN, son of Daniel and Susanah Smith Morgan, was born in Jackson County, September 5, 1841. In December 1867, he married Mary Ann Butler who died May 6, 1883. In 1885 he married Mary Trodgen, at Smithville. Mr. Morgan attended Burritt College and later studied law. He was elected Attorney General in 1870 and served eight years. He was elected to the State Senate in 1880 and made Speaker of that body. Mr. Morgan was a 32nd degree Mason and in 1892, was Grand Master of Tennessee. He was a Democrat and a member of the Church of Christ. He moved to Cookeville in 1887 and resided here until his death, August 20, 1900.

ALFRED ALGOOD, son of Joel and Nancy Algood, was born

in Wilson County, May 28, 1885. He attended the East Tennessee University at Knoxville, and later took a course in law at Vanderbilt University. He was elected Attorney General in 1886, and served eight years, declining a second term. He married Miss Lula Williams, of Louisville, Ky. Mr. Algood was an able and conscientious lawyer, a Christian gentleman, and a citizen of the highest type. He was a leading member of the M. E. Church, South, and was also prominent in the councils of the Democratic party. He died at his home in Cookeville, January 25, 1925, leaving a record full of inspiration for every young man.

CHARLES HENRY WHITNEY. Among the first to come to Cookeville from a distant state was Charles H. Whitney, of Marshall, Minnesota, who moved here with his family in 1887. A few months later he purchased the Hitchcock place, which he greatly improved. For several years he was actively engaged in real-estate and contracting business. He was a public spirited citizen and was ever ready to do his part and more for the betterment of his adopted town and state. Col. Whitney, as he was familiarly known, was a Republican in politics and an active and powerful leader in his party. He was postmaster at Cookeville from 1907 to 1910 and his administration was one of the best the town ever had. In 1896 he ran for Congress against Benton McMillin and received a record-breaking vote. He was a member of the Church of Christ, a Mason and a Knight of Pythias. He died December 25, 1912, lacking only a few days of reaching his 75th year.

Just as worthy of notice, if not quite as conspicuous in public affairs, were these other able and highly esteemed citizens, namely:

Capt. H. H. Dillard, Major J. C. Freeze, Dr. J. M. Goodpasture, Charles Burton, Sr., Stephen, D. Burton, Henry P. Davis, Capt. C. J. Davis, Josiah Jared, Capt. J. H. Curtis, Moses A. Jared, Samuel Young, H. B. C. Vaden, Dr. William Farmer, Dr. F. M. Amonett, Dr. Richard Fane, Dr. Wm. Robinson, James M. Douglass, Sr., Isaac D. Reagan, David H. Nichols, William Burton, Alex Burton, Jesse Arnold, Peter Young, Martin Sims, John Terry, Elder William Kuykendall, Alvin W. Boyd, Houston S. Boyd, T. L. Denny, William G. Davis, Abraham Ford, Charles R. Ford,

A HISTORY OF PUTNAM COUNTY

William J. Isbell, Columbus Marchbanks, Holland Denton, J. H. McCulley, Wade Jones, Dr. J. P. Martin, A. R. Massa, Rev. W. H. Carr, Milton M. Owen, Rev. Simeon K. Phillips, Richard F. Pippin, Dr. Simeon Hinds, Jack Ray, Joseph Riddle, A. A. Reagan, Capt. Samuel G. Slaughter, Anderson Sloan, Capt. Walton Smith, Sanford Stamps, Henry C. Taylor, Jeremiah M. Whitson, John H. Dowell, J. H. Moore, David L. Dow, W. T. Bockman, J. C. Bockman, William H. Walker, Pleas. Bohanon, Campbell Bohanon, Alvin Wirt, J. J. Whittaker, A. Bryant, Charles Bradford, Henry M. Nicholas, Thomas Pointer, Rev. T. J. Clouse, Rev. Henry Johnson, T. J. Lee, Z. T. Hinds, Capt. William P. Chapin, E. D. Staley, John Epperson, Capt. W. A. Crawford, Gid H. Lowe, Rev. M. Judd, T. A. Head, James McKinley, J. F. Thompson.

Recent Deaths—During the last two years death has taken heavy toll among our well known citizens. We make especial mention of these: Esq. J. Ridley Douglass, a prominent attorney and long active in public affairs; H. S. Barnes, a young lawyer of much promise and ability; Philip M. Smith, long active and conspicuous in the mercantile world; John W. Chilcutt, J. H. Quarles and John E. Wall, long residents of Cookeville and among our best citizens. Thomas Holloway, R. C. and R. L. Walker, three leading business men of Monterey.

We give here short Biographical Sketches of a few of the leading citizens of the County, representing different professions and occupations. That the people in every district are alive to progressiveness is shown by the wonderful progress the County is making in farming, manufacturing, better schools and better roads.

ROBERT L. FARLEY, born at Newark, White County, October 20, 1869. He attended public schools and Doyle College. He married Miss Florence Fowler. Mr. Farley was first book-keeper then Cashier of the old Bank of Cookeville for many years. He is at present interested in several large manufacturing enterprises, in which he has been eminently successful. He is a Democrat but has never sought office. Member of the Church of Christ, Mason and President of the Cookeville Lions Club. Was a

A HISTORY OF PUTNAM COUNTY

Colonel on the staff of Gov. Rye. Mr. Farley can always be counted upon to do his full duty in every undertaking of a worthy nature.

A. GILLEM MAXWELL, born near Cookeville, September 20, 1866. On September 14, 1890, he married Miss Nannie C. Washburn, who died in 1912. On March 6, 1921, he married Miss Vena May Martin. Mr. Maxwell began his business life as a commercial traveler—and there was no better on the road. Entering business for himself, he made a success of every enterprise he attempted. Today he owns more real-estate than any other individual in Cookeville. He and Mr. Farley own a controlling interest in numerous spoke mills, veneering mills, flour mills, etc. Mr. Maxwell is a Democrat and a member of the Church of Christ. Was a Colonel on the staff of Gov. Roberts. One of the most progressive and public spirited citizens of the county.

JOHN THOMAS MOORE, M. D., born near Dry Valley, November 6, 1876. Received his M. D. degree at University of Tennessee. Post Graduate from New York University. Married to Miss Dorcas Pennock, who died in 1908. Married to Miss Amice Crews in 1913. Dr. Moore lives at Algood and enjoys a large practice. Interested in every movement to build the County. He is a Scottish Rite Mason and Shriner. Vice-President of the State Medical Society and Ex-President Upper Cumberland Medical Society. Formerly President Bank of Algood, Director Tennessee Hermitage National Bank at Nashville. Director Gainesboro Telephone Co., Maxwell-Hill Grocery Co., and connected with many other business and public enterprises.

JAMES NEWTON KING, born at Paint Rock, Roane County, Tennessee, March 15, 1850. He is a Democrat, a Methodist and a Mason. Has been Chairman of the County Court, and has served three terms in the Legislature. Before his retirement Mr. King taught thirty-two years and was a very popular and efficient teacher. He is a progressive farmer and interested in everything looking to the betterment of his fellow citizens. His first wife died several years ago. A few years later he married Miss Annie M. Smith.

MR. AND MRS. JERE WHITSON

JEREMIAH WHITSON, born one mile south of Cookeville, March 19, 1853. On March 19, 1872, he married Miss Parizetta Frances Terry. When but a lad of sixteen years he struck out for himself and secured employment in the store of Freeze & Mills. He established a small general store of his own in Jackson County in 1871, but soon sold it and, in 1872, associated with J. H. Moore, opened a general store in Cookeville. In 1875, Mr. Whitson moved to Jeremiah and entered upon a prosperous career. Moving back to Cookeville in 1890, Mr. Whitson soon became actively identified with every worthy public movement and has continued to be one of our foremost citizens. The Jere Whitson Hardware Co., established in 1896 does a large business, wholesale and retail. Mr. Whitson has also engaged extensively in farming and real estate with characteristic success. In politics he is a Democrat, but has never held public office, although always an active party worker. An elder and recognized leader in the Church of Christ. The founding of Dixie College was due primarily to his earnest and persistent labor.

A HISTORY OF PUTNAM COUNTY

JEFFERSON FRANKLIN DYER, M. D., was born five miles west of Cookeville, July 6, 1848. Married Miss Elizabeth Seawell, May 15, 1877, who died October 20, 1891. Married Miss Avo Goodpasture, June 10, 1894. Finished his education at Vanderbilt Medical College. Was County Health Officer eight years. Dr. Dyer is a Democrat, an elder in the Presbyterian Church, U. S. A., a Mason and charter member of the Cookeville lodge of Odd Fellows. He was on the committee to rebuild Washington Academy, Courthouse and the Presbyterian Church, U. S. A. He has been practicing medicine in Cookeville since 1878.

JOHN BALLARD SPRINGS MARTIN, M. D., was born at McMinnville, Tenn., March 19, 1848. He was married May 26, 1875, to Miss Lillie D. Crutcher. Attended Cumberland Institute, Dibrell Academy, University of Nashville and Vanderbilt Medical College. Dr. Martin is a Democrat, a Mason and a member of the Church of Christ. He has taken high degrees in York and Scottish Rite Masonry. Was the first druggist to do business in Cookeville, back in 1874 to 1878. He moved to Cookeville in 1873. Began the practice of Medicine in 1878.

WILLIAM HARDIN RAGLAND, M. D., was born in Smith County, September 22, 1842. Completed his education at Vanderbilt Medical College and has practiced extensively in Jackson and Putnam Counties. Moved to Cookeville about twenty-five years ago. Dr. Ragland is a Confederate veteran, a Democrat and a Methodist. He was married three times and has seven grown children. He is a son of Dr. William Ragland, a well known physician of his day. At eighty-three he is in splendid health. He retired from practice of medicine several years ago.

LEMUEL RUCKS McCLAIN, M. D., was born at Clarksville, Ark., December 29, 1844. Married Miss Sarah Emily Burton at White Plaines, this County, on November 19, 1867. She died September 1, 1910. Dr. McClain attended the Missouri Medical College, at St. Louis. He is a life long Democrat, a Methodist in belief, and has been a prominent Odd Fellow since 1873 and a Mason since 1869. He has been Secretary of the Odd Fellows lodge of Cookeville for more than thirty years, and through his untiring efforts the Odd Fellows built their home two years ago.

DR. J. F. DYER

DR. J. B. S. MARTIN

DR. W. H. RAGLAND

DR. L. R. McCLAIN

OSCAR K. HOLLADAY, born at Pekin, Putnam County, November 6, 1876. Married Miss Margaret Denny, September 17, 1902. Completed his education at Cumberland University. Mr. Holladay is recognized as an able lawyer and a leading member of the Cookeville bar. He served two terms in the State Senate and was author of the Holladay Bill, which was the beginning of prohibition in Tennessee. He is one of the leading Democrats of the state, a Scottish Rite Mason, and a steward in the M. E. Church, South.

JOSEPH DANIEL HARRIS, born in Putnam County, June 28, 1871. Graduate of University of Chattanooga. Married Miss Martha Anderson in 1891. After her death, married Miss Gertrude Gentry in 1911. Taught school for several years and then prepared for the ministery. He is a member of the Methodist Episcopal Church, of Holston Conference. Rev. Harris has been a leading citizen of Baxter for many years. Founder of Baxter Seminary, Chariman of first board of Trustees and financial agent for four years. Has served as pastor in five states, built sixteen churches and parsonages in Middle Tennessee. At present engaged in evangelistic work.

JESSE PEYTON TERRY, born July 7, 1885, near Cookeville. Graduate of University of Tennessee. One of the leading dentists of Cookeville. Before moving to Cookeville was Mayor of Algood, 1919-20. Thirty-second degree Mason, Knight Templar and Shriner. Married to Miss Alice Smith, September 16, 1913. While a citizen of Algood he contributed liberally in building a public road from Algood to Monterey. An active member of the Cookeville Lions Club and Putnam County Shriners Club. Member of the American and Tennessee Dental Associations.

JEFF ESTEL WALL, born near Club Springs, Smith County, Tenn., August 15, 1888. Married Miss Vera Jenkins, of Cookeville. Mr. Wall is a Gospel Singer and is making a great success. His services are sought all over the Southern States. He is a Democrat, Mason and member of the Methodist Church. He is one of the general singers of the Southern Methodist Church, but assists other denominations when called.

HON. O. K. HOLLADAY

REV. J. D. HARRIS

DR. J. P. TERRY

JEFF E. WALL

A HISTORY OF PUTNAM COUNTY

LAWRENCE GRACE, born in Christian County, Kentucky. Graduate of Southern Normal School, Bowling Green, Ky. Married Miss Vinnie Gentry, May 7, 1917. Alderman of Baxter for past six years. President of Baxter Bank. Has promoted many successful enterprises. Mr. Grace is one of Baxters most progressive citizens and gives much time to public enterprises. He is a member of the Methodist Church, a Mason, Odd Fellow and a Charter member of the Booster Club of Baxter.

ELMER LINCOLN WIRT, born in Olmstead County, Minn., June 5, 1863. Married to Miss Catherine B. Diamond, July 3, 1887. Mr. Wirt is Editor and Publisher of the Putnam County Herald, which paper he established twenty years ago. Mr. Wirt was elected by the Democratic party to the lower house of the Legislature in 1914. He is the author of the bill creating Tennessee Polytechnic Institute, mentioned in a preceeding chapter. He is a member of the Methodist Church.

STEPHEN HAYDEN YOUNG, born at White Plains, Putnam County, October 13, 1874. Finished his education at the University of Tennessee. Married to Miss Effie Boyd, October 3, 1903. Member of the Church of Christ. Mr. Young helped organize the Gainesboro Telephone Company and has been with them ever since. He is now Treasurer of the Company. A citizen of the highest order, unassuming but ready at all times to give for the betterment of the County. Mr. Young has been a citizen of Cookeville for many years and deals extensively in real-estate.

CHARLES BEECHER GENTRY, born October 13, 1888, two miles south of Cookeville. Graduate of Grandview Normal and Tennessee Polytechnic Institute. Married Miss Elizabeth Taylor. County Superintendent of Putnam County. Under his administration the school term has been lengthened from five to eight months. Mr. Gentry is a member of the Baptist Church, a Mason and prominent in the ranks of the Republican party.

LAWRENCE GRACE

HON. E. L. WIRT

S. H. YOUNG

C. BEECHER GENTRY

A HISTORY OF PUTNAM COUNTY

ROBERT LEE RICHARDSON, born near Baxter, April 6, 1882. Completed his education at Baxter Seminary. Married, September 25, 1902 to Miss Rebecca McHenry. Engaged in banking, insurance and farming. Vice-President Baxter Bank, Alderman of Baxter, and Vice-President Business Men's Booster Club. A Mason, I. O. O. F., M. W. A., and a member of the Baptist Church. Mr. Richardson is one of Putnam County's most progressive citizens.

WALTER RALEIGH CARLEN, born in Buffalo Valley, February 23, 1879. Educated in the Cookeville schools. Married Miss Fannie Richmond, September 16, 1900. He has been Clerk and Master for eleven years. Vice-President Citizens Bank and Coca-Cola Bottling works. Mr. Carlen is one of the leading Democrats of this section, member of the Methodist Church and an Odd Fellow.

OAKLEY D. MASSA, born in the 16th district of Putnam County. Married Miss Mattie M. Stanton, January 1, 1911. Mr. Massa is a member of the Jere Whitson Hardware Co., Secretary and Treasurer of the Putnam County Agricultural Fair. He is a Republican, a Methodist and a Mason. For the past few years Mr. Massa has been very active in securing business enterprises for Cookeville. He is an active member of the Cookeville Lion's Club.

WILLIAM GROVER ANDERSON, born in Boma, Tenn., March 24, 1889. Married Miss Lillian Lee, July 21, 1915. Engaged in wholesale and retail hardware. He has built several large business houses at Baxter. Has been Mayor of Baxter. He is a member of the County Board of Education, a member of all the branches of Masonry and a devoted member of the Baptist Church. Mr. Anderson is one of Baxter's most valuable citizens.

W. R. CARLEN

R. L. RICHARDSON

OAKLEY D. MASSA

W. G. ANDERSON

A HISTORY OF PUTNAM COUNTY

ERNEST HOUSTON BOYD, born October 1, 1880. Finished his education at Cumberland University, where he also graduated in law. Married to Miss Mattie Ragland, August 21, 1912. Has held the offices of County Superintendent and County Attorney and at present Attorney-General of the Fifth Judicial Circuit. Mr. Boyd is a Democrat, and an elder in the Presbyterian Church, U. S. A. He is Deputy Grand Master, Grand Lodge, I. O. O. F., of Tennessee.

WILLIAM A. HENSLEY. was born near Gainesboro, October 28, 1883. Attended Mont Vale Academy. Married Miss Nevada E. Mayberry, May 14, 1905. Mr. Hensley is the present Mayor of Cookeville. He is a Democrat and a member of Gov. Peay's staff. He is a member of the Church of Christ, an Odd Fellow and a Thirty-second degree Mason. Mayor Hens'ey is a business man of ability and has been identified with several large enterprises. He is an enthusiastic advocate of civic improvement.

JAMES NATHANIEL COX, born in Gainesboro, February 9, 1876. Graduate of the University of Tennessee. Married to Miss Mary Young, April 7, 1897. Was one of the organizers of the Gainesboro Telephone Co. Has been Vice-President and General Manager of the Company for twenty-eight years. Under his management the Company has enjoyed wonderful growth. Serving his second term as State Democratic Committeeman for Fourth District. Member of the Church of Christ. Active in all branches of the Masonic order. Ex-President Lions Club of Cookeville.

BEECHER CUMMINS HUDDLESTON, born April 19, 1870. Married Miss Mary F. Buck, January 7, 1894, who died December 14, 1895. On February 18, 1900, he married Mrs. Ruth Walker. Mr. Huddleston is a successful farmer and interested in all progressive movements. He has been a Justice of the Peace since 1906. Present Chairman of the County Executive Committee. He is an Odd Fellow and a steward in the Salem M. E. Church, South.

HON. E. H. BOYD

MAYOR W. A. HENSLEY

JAMES N. COX

B. C. HUDDLESTON

REV. H. L. UPPERMAN   GROVER C. BOYD

HARRY LEE UPPERMAN, born in Baltimore, Maryland, June 23, 1895. Graduate of Syracuse University, Syracuse, New York. Married to Miss Elma Elizabeth Clark, of Williamsport, Pa. Minister and teacher, Pastor for six years in New York state. At present President Baxter Seminary. Rev. Upperman is a member of the Methodist Episcopal Church, Mason and President Baxter Booster's Club. He traveled and studied abroad in 1922.

GROVER C. BOYD, born in Cookeville, September 30, 1891. Attended Cookeville schools, Lebanon Law School and Georgetwn University, LL. B., 1916. Served abroad in the World War. Began practice Cookeville, July, 1919. Mr. Boyd is a Democrat, a Mason and a Presbyterian, U. S. A. He is a leading member of the American Legion, and a lawyer of ability. After his return from the war, Mr. Boyd practiced law for two years with Col. B. G. Adcock, but has recently been associated in practice with his brother, Hon. E. H. Boyd.

A HISTORY OF PUTNAM COUNTY

DAVID C. WILHITE, born in the 11th district of White County, Tennessee, January 22, 1867. He received his education in the public schools and at Pleasant Hill. Married in 1893 to Miss Narcissa Whittaker. Mr. Wilhite is a Democrat, member of the Church of Christ, and a Deacon in that Church. He is at present Chairman of County Board of Education, member of City Board of Education. President First National Bank of Cookeville and a member of the Federal Bank System. Mr. Wilhite moved to Putnam County in 1893 and bought the Isaac Buck farm three miles south of Cookeville, later he moved to Algood where he served as President of the Algood Bank for three years. He is one of Putnam County's most successful business men.

WILLIAM BRADLEY RAY, born at Beaver Hill, Overton County, February 29, 1860. Married Miss Susie Jones Turner, February 23, 1887. Attended Cumberland Institute and Elmwood Institute. He is a Democrat, a steward in the M. E. Church, South, a K. of P., and an Odd Fellow. Mr. Ray has been President of the Bank of Monterey for twenty years, and has engaged extensively in manufacturing, farming and real estate, and is a Director in several large corporations.

HUGH SMITH HARGIS, born in Granville, January 30, 1875. Attended public and private schools. Married Miss Vallie Lee Holleman in 1899. Mr. Hargis is engaged in various enterprises. He is Cashier of the Citizens Bank, Vice-President Coca-Cola Co., and President Cookeville Ice Co. Owns big dairy farms in Putnam and Davidson Counties. He is one of the City Commissioners, a Democrat, a Mason, a Methodist and member of the Cookeville Lions Club.

JOHN W. WELCH, born two miles south of Monterey, in February, 1859. Married Miss Julia Ford, August 1878. Mr. Welch is Mayor of Monterey, and is prominently indentified with its business interests. He is a K. of P., and an Odd Fellow. He is President of the Bill's Branch Coal Company, and also the Monterey Realty Company. He has dealt extensively in lumber and real estate for the past 25 years, and owns several thousand acres of valuable coal and timber lands.

CARSON E. HAMPTON, born in Overton County, May 14, 1896. Married Miss Mabel Copeland, December 15, 1919. Mayor of Algood. Cashier of the Bank of Algood since he was twenty-one years old. Is a Democrat, a Methodist and Shriner. One of Algood's progressive young business men.

ROBERT PERRY MORGAN, born in Jackson County, January 15, 1867. Married Miss Viola Davis, January 15, 1892. Mr. Morgan is a Democrat, a K. of P., and a Cumberland Presbyterian in belief. He has never held public office, except alderman of Cookeville about twenty years ago. He moved here about thirty-five years ago and has been actively engaged in the produce business, retail and wholesale. His is the oldest business concern in Cookeville.

ROBERT BIRD CAPSHAW, born in Warren County, December 13, 1855. Married Miss Alice G. Whitson, December 2, 1883. Mr. Capshaw read law under Judge B. M. Webb, and was admitted to the bar. He has resided in Cookeville since July 12, 1873, and has enjoyed a large and lucrative practice. He is a member of the Church of Christ, a Democrat and a member of the Lion's Club. He is at present a Justice of the Peace.

JOE HAYWOOD JARED, born in Rock Spring Valley, in 1861. Married Miss Laura Shields, in 1887. After her death, he married Miss Ina McCaleb. Mr. Jared is a prominent Democrat but has never held public office. He is a Methodist in belief. He has been engaged extensively in farming and timber business, and owns one of the largest and most valuable farms in the county.

HARVEY DENTON WHITSON, born near Cookeville, May 15, 1870. He married Miss Etta Farley. Attended school at Pleasant Hill and Alpine, Tennessee. Was County Superintendent two terms and is serving his fifteenth year in the office of County Judge. He is a Democrat, a Steward in the M. E. Church, South, and an Odd Fellow. He has been President of the Home Telephone Co., and also the Farmers Fire Insurance Co.

NORMAN MASSA, born near Cookeville, April 12, 1881. Received his education in the public schools. Married to Miss Elizabeth Brown in 1901. Has been in the mercantile business since a young man. Register of the County from 1910-14. He has been prominent in the Republican party of Tennessee for many years. Postmaster at Cookeville and Custodian of the Federal building. Member of State Executive Committtee, Chair-

A HISTORY OF PUTNAM COUNTY

man of County Committee, and was Secretary of the Executive Committee of the 4th Congressional District for four years. Member of the Methodist Church, Knight Templar, Shriner, and member of the Lion's Club of Cookeville.

POTTER M. GREENWOOD, born in Overton County, January 7, 1850. Married Miss Lucy Peek, who died January 2, 1891. Mr. Greenwood is a Democrat and a Cumberland Presbyterian. He has never held office and has been engaged principally in farming with marked success.

JOHN CLAUDE DARWIN, born near Gainesboro, October 23, 1882. Completed his education at Joseph W. Allen College, Carthage, Tennessee. Married Miss Clio Draper, August 6, 1915. Moved to Cookeville fifteen years ago and organized the mercantile firm of Jenkins & Darwin Bros. Was City Commissioner of Finance for three years. Mr. Darwin is a Democrat, a Presbyterian, U. S. A., and a member of the Lion's Club.

THOMAS D. FORD, born in Cookeville, June 19, 1862. Married Miss Virgina Bell Birdwell, November 27, 1887. His father, C. R. Ford, was one of the first settlers of Cookeville and Putnam County. He is a member of the Church of Christ, a Democrat and a Mason. He has been in the fire insurance business for many years. Mr. Ford is the oldest citizen of Cookeville who was born here.

WILLIAM CARSON OFFICER, M. D., born in Overton County in 1880. Married Miss Lula Miller in 1907. Graduate in medicine University of Tennessee and Tulane University. Practiced since 1902. Member Church of Christ, Mason and Odd Fellow. Head of Officer's Sanitorium, near Monterey. Stockholder in other enterprises.

ORREN EDWARD CAMERON, born twelve miles south of Sparta, May 1, 1883. Finished his education at Burritt College. Married Miss Bessie Arnold, in 1910. Cashier of the First National Bank of Cookeville, City Commissioner of Finance. Mr. Cameron is a Republican, an Odd Fellow and a member of the Presbyterian Church, U. S. A., and Lion's Club.

ABRAHAM POTEET WELCH, born near Monterey in 1881. Married Miss Daisy Andrews, in 1900. Mr. Welch is an able minister of the Nazarene faith, and has been pastor of the

A HISTORY OF PUTNAM COUNTY

Monterey church for twenty years. He also has large business interests in manufacturing and real estate. He is Vice-President of the Union Bank and Trust Company, of Monterey.

LINNIE MILAN BULLINGTON, born December 16, 1884, in Gentry, Tennessee. Graduate of Cumberland University Law School. Married April 12, 1915, to Miss Cora Allison. Has been engaged in the practice of law in Cookeville since 1909. Commissioner of Finance of Cookeville 1920-24. Member of Methodist Episcopal Church, South. During his term as Commissioner, Cookeville's one hundred thousand dollar Grammar School was erected also the light plant. He gave four years of his time to Cookeville in an efficent and pains-taking way. Mr. Bullington is a strong advocate of good roads and better schools.

ROBERT LEE MADDUX, born in Buffalo Valley, June 26, 1889. Married Miss Lorelle Adcock, December 29, 1914. Mr. Maddux has been engaged in the mercantile business in Cookeville for several years. He is a Democrat, a Knight Templar and a Shriner. He is a member of the Church of Christ. Secretary and Treasurer Tennessee Fox Hunter's Association. An extensive dealer in real-estate and a strong believer in Cookeville and Putnam County.

VIRGIL C. ALLISON, born in the 8th district of Putnam County in 1892. Graduated in law at Cumberland University. Married Anna Copeland. Mr. Allison has been living in Monterey since 1901. Is a lawyer of ability and a member of the County Court. Saw service in France during the World War. A Republican, a Mason and an Odd Fellow. One of Monterey's wide-awake citizens.

HARVEY DILLARD McCULLEY, born near Cookeville, April 27, 1871. Educated at Alpine Institute and Yeargan Select School. Married Miss Minnie Phrasier, March 23, 1902. Mr. McCulley has been a teacher in the public schools of the county for many years. He is President of the Putnam County Teachers' Association, Odd Fellow and a member of the Presbyterian Church, U. S. A.

JAMES A. CARLEN, born in the 11th Civil district in 1854. Married Miss Minerva Huddleston, in 1878. Engaged in farming until he moved to Cookeville in 1880. Is a prominent Democrat and held the office of Circuit and Criminal Court Clerk for twelve years. He is a Methodist and a Mason.

A HISTORY OF PUTNAM COUNTY

LEX DYER, M. D., born in Cookeville, December 12, 1882. Married Miss Audra Haynes, April 11, 1914. Graduate University of Nashville Medical School. County Health Officer since 1914. Dr. Dyer is associated in practice with his father, Dr. J. F. Dyer. He is a Democrat, a Mason, an Odd Fellow and a Presbyterian, U. S. A.

ALFRED WHITTEN MAXWELL, born in the 17th district of Putnam County, May 3, 1886. Married Miss Avo Worley in 1906. Engaged in the general mercantile business at Baxter. Was Justice of the Peace for six years. Mr. Maxwell is a Republican, Odd Fellow, and a Methodist. A progressive and public spirited citizen.

DOW E. SLAGLE, born in Buffalo Valley, Tennessee, September 5, 1872. Attended school at Washington Academy. Married Miss Sallie Williams. Mr. Slagle is a bookkeeper by profession. Was County Trustee for four years. Supervisor of Federal Census 1920, and one term as Deputy State Fire Marshal. He is well known over the county having been an active worker in the Democratic party for several years. Member of the Methodist Church and a Mason.

ALEXANDER PLEAS BARNES, born near Cookeville, about sixty years ago. Attended public school at Cookeville. Married Miss Fannie Terry in 1886. Mayor of Cookeville from 1921-23. During his term of office as Mayor, he built a new light plant, new school building and made many other improvements. Mr. Barnes is a Democrat, a member of the Church of Christ and a member the Lion's Club.

DOW ALLISON ENSOR, born in the 11th district of Putnam County, August 5, 1875. Educated in the public schools and Yeargan Select School. Taught school for eight years. Married to Miss Lizzie Rash twenty years ago. Minister of the M. E. Church, South. Mason, Odd Fellow and Knight of Pythias. Mr. Ensor joined the Tennessee Annual Conference of the M. E. Church, South, in 1902. He is known to practically every citizen of the county as a strong advocate of better schools and better citizenship. He is now living on a farm near Cookeville.

JAMES MONROE HATFIELD, born at Livingston, September 21, 1871. Married Miss Willie May Barnes. Attended Cookeville schools and Peabody College. He is a member of the Church of Christ, an Odd Fellow and a Democrat. As County Superintendent of Schools (1911-21) he inaugurated many reforms and improvements. He has been President of the Public School Officer's Association of Tennessee. He has taught in some of the leading schools in this part of the State. At present, he is a teacher in the Tennessee Polytechnic Institute.

JAMES ANDREW ISBELL, born in Buffalo Valley, May 20, 1870. Received his education in the public schools, Washington Academy and Chattanooga University. He was married to Miss Cora F. Leftwich, March 3, 1900. For twenty years Mr. Isbell has been engaged in the manufacture of handles. He moved his large factory to Cookeville two years ago from Baxter. He was President of the Baxter Bank for several years, also Chairman of the Trustees of Baxter Seminary. He has always been a good roads enthusiast and was Secretary of the Western Division on good roads about fifteen years ago. Is a member of the Lion's Club of Cookeville, Odd Fellow and a steward in the Methodist Church.

ZEBEDEE L. SHIPLEY, M. D., born near Cookeville, June 15, 1873. Attended Alpine Institute and Grant University Medical School, (Chattanooga). Married Miss Florence Barnes, December 12, 1902. He is a Democrat, an Odd Fellow, Mason and a member of several Medical Societies. Dr. Shipley taught school before taking up the study of his profession. He is a member of the Church of Christ and Vice-President of the Cookeville Lion's Club.

FRED H. WHITE, born December 21, 1859, in Bambridge, New York. Finished his education at Minneapolis Business College. Married Miss Millie A. Whitney, December 31, 1888. Moved to Cookeville in 1901. Has one of the largest farms in the County, about three miles of Cookeville. Mr. White is a progressive citizen and runs his farm by the most successful methods.

JOHN G. DUKE, born at Lancaster, Smith County, July 18, 1848. Married Miss Mary Gentry, August 19, 1875. Mr. Duke moved to Cookeville forty-eight years ago. and has helped to build the town. He has been in the mercantile business for forty-five years. Mr. Duke is a prominent Republican and was Postmaster of Cookeville for two terms. He is a Mason, K. of P., and a Presbyterian, U. S. A.

OSCAR LAFAYETTE GARRETT, born at Old Monroe, Overton County, November 1, 1880. Married Miss L. Robbins at Monterey, 1904. Has been in the barber business since 1903. He is a Democrat, a member of the Church of Christ, a 32nd degree Mason and a Shriner.

MIKE MOORE, born near Cookeville, in 1856. Married Miss Mary Terry, in 1876, who died in 1896. In 1898 he married Mrs. Linnie Selby. Mr. Moore was for many years a leading merchant of the town but retired several years ago. He is a Democrat, a Methodist and a Mason.

PETER YOUNG JARED, born on Big Indian Creek, June 1, 1866. Married Miss Sallie Burton, November 8, 1887. Mr. Jared is a prominent Democrat and held the office of Circuit Court Clerk for two terms. He is engaged in farming and lives in the 11th Civil district, where he has always resided except when in office. He is a Methodist and a Mason.

THOMAS JESSE CLARK, born in the 3rd district of Putnam County, September 19, 1866. Attended the public schools. Was married June 19, 1887, to Miss Julia Milligan. Has been engaged in the successful manufacture of lumber for many years. As a citizen of Algood for the past eighteen years he has devoted time and money in building the town. Was Secretary and Treasurer of Pennock-Walter M'f'g. Co., for seventeen years. This firm practically built Algood. Now member of the Clark Lumber Co. Mr. Clark is one of Putnam County's most progressive and substantial citizens.

HENRY CLAY MARTIN, M. D., born in Spencer, July 9, 1853. Married Miss Lou Shields, in 1877, who died July 8, 1911. On July 28, 1912, he married Mrs. Hettie Sims. Dr. Martin is a graduate of the Vanderbilt Medical School and has practiced in Cookeville since 1884. He is a member of the Church of Christ, a Mason, an Odd Fellow, a Woodman and a Democrat.

WILLIAM LEWIS JOHNSON, born November 8, 1876, in the 11th district of Putnam County. Finished his education at Pleasant Hill Academy. Married to Miss Lula M. Johnson of

A HISTORY OF PUTNAM COUNTY

Cumberland County, May 4, 1907. Member of the Church of Christ, and a leading Odd Fellow, also member of the Baxter Business Men's Club. Mr. Johnson has the largest nursery in this part of the state, located near Baxter. He established the first nursery in the County. Baxter, his home town, always calls on him for assistance in putting over enterprises and he is always ready with his time and money.

HERBIE J. SHANKS, born at Sparta, June 8, 1883. Married Miss Elizabeth M. Maddux. Has lived in Cookeville practically all of his life. Mr. Shanks is a Democrat and a deacon in the Baptist Church. He has been engaged in the hotel and lumber business for several years. He is a wide-awake citizen. He is a member of the Lion's Club.

VAN D. NUNALLY, born in Lafayette, Tennessee, July 15, 1887. Graduate of University of Chattanooga, (Athens Department). Engaged in the Drug business at Baxter. Has been Mayor of Baxter for four years. A Republican in politics and a member of the Modern Woodmen of America. Under his administration as Mayor, Baxter has become one of the best advertised towns on the Tennessee Central.

MADISON C. FARLEY, born in the 8th district of Putnam County in 1858. Mr. Farley moved to Ditty, in the 16th district, forty-three years ago. He was in the mercantile business there for ten years. Road Overseer for a number of years and Supervisor of roads for two years. He has been Postmaster of Ditty for twenty years and was Justice of the Peace from that district for nine years. He is a Democrat.

WALTER STEPHEN McCLAIN, D. O., born near Cookeville, August 24, 1868. Married Miss Minnie Avery, March 15, 1897. Graduate Lebanon Law School and Southern School of Osteopathy. Has also done newspaper work. Democrat and Odd Fellow.

QUIMBY DYER, born in Cookeville, July 3, 1880. Married Miss Etta Johnson, June 15, 1904. Served in Legislature of 1907. Democrat, Presbyterian, U. S. A., Shriner, Lion's Club. Engaged in newspaper work and real estate for past twenty years.

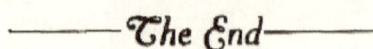

The End

www.ingramcontent.com/pod-product-compliance
Lightning Source LLC
Chambersburg PA
CBHW020654300426
44112CB00007B/371